4 Phases of Spiritual Warfare:

Navigate Sabotage
Build SUCCESS

ENDORSEMENTS

Becky and I met over a pizza. Sometimes we walk around a corner and get hit in the face with a 2x4 that rearranges our teeth. And other times, equally as dramatic, we walk through a door and meet the person we'll marry and have 4 kids with. This was mine and Becky's start. The pizza and kids, not the 2x4. But the 2x4 metaphor is relevant here as most of us go through life asleep. Not paying attention to the world around us, especially the spiritual world. Having known Becky since just after I picked up that pizza, I've seen her walk out her life in ways most have not. Sometimes with sauce on her shirt and sometimes with fervent prayer overcoming tremendous obstacles and challenges through her faith. I've seen Becky when she had MUCH more faith than I did. Sometimes the situation was simple and sometimes was serious and complex. On one occasion we had an old van. We lived in Florida, and the AC quit on us in the summer. Not good for having kids you needed to cart around. The quote was over $1,000 to repair it. My mentality was, roll down the windows and drive faster. Becky prayed and told me that she believed we should go to the Toyota dealership and ask them what they could do. I said no, because who gets favor from an auto dealership? Well, she went, being that I wouldn't. And they not only reduced the price but gave us the option to put it on a payment plan with no interest! This is a small example of the way Becky has lived her life. Approaching it through prayer and simple obedience. As such, she has produced 4 incredible productive adults, a business helping others develop their faith, and the realization of worthwhile hopes and dreams. Something many of us cannot relate to because we live our lives asleep looking for how to avoid the 2x4 versus looking for how to live by faith. **– Jay Harmon**, husband

Only a fool would rush into battle without weapons or protection. As Christians, we are in a combat zone every day. We don't get to choose whether we want to be warriors. The clash between light and darkness is escalating dramatically. We have to choose to prepare, strategize, and use wisdom and discernment. If we think we can be pacifists and be victorious, we are deceived. God has not left us defenseless – quite the contrary is true. He has given us everything we need to succeed in overcoming the enemy. We have to suit up, show up, go up, and grow up in order to win. You will value *4 Phases of Spiritual Warfare* as an essential tool in this process.

Becky Harmon is a woman on a mission to build the Kingdom of God by equipping others to walk in confident strength in their God-given identity. Becky and I met as intercessors on a weekly prayer call to cover a church planting team in the war zone of Miami, FL. Soon after, we became prayer partners – weekly covering our families, businesses, ministries, and lives with militant prayer. Our friendship of nearly 10 years has resulted in doing both business and ministry workshops together and seeing people get set free to grow into the fullness of their destiny. Becky is one of the most strategic intercessors I know. It is fitting and timely for her to encapsulate her story, experience, and years of Bible study and prayer into a manual for Spiritual Warfare.

Becky is boldly authentic. She speaks the truth in a spirit of love. She will challenge you to think and provoke you to grow in your relationship with Christ. She does not sugar coat the truth. If you want straight advice that qualifies you to be effective in the battles you are facing, you have the right book in your hands. Becky is a spiritual general in God's army and is committed to helping others achieve breakthrough. You will never be bored as you read and partner with Becky. Buckle up – she will take you higher, deeper, and further than you thought possible. **– Beverly Lewis**, Speaker, Trainer, Author of *Win from Within: The Heart of Success and Significance*

Becky has a rare ability to see the giftings and callings in others even before they themselves see it. She not only calls them out but encourages and assists others to begin walking in their calling.

I have been walking very closely with Becky for almost 20 years and have continuously watched her say "yes" to God in the face of her own fears and insecurities. Who she is today is rooted in the years and years of submission and repentance to God through daily quiet times. She is marked by her authenticity, as she regularly shares her past and present struggles, and is willing to receive and listen to godly advice. It has truly been a privilege to walk with Becky as she has held me accountable and encouraged me throughout my walk with God. Becky is one of the greatest blessings in my life.

Years ago, I accompanied Becky on a mission trip to Uganda, Africa. I watched as she ministered to a group of timid, very closed teenage girls, most of who had been sexually abused. As she followed the leading of the Holy Spirit and shared her own personal pain, these girls slowly stepped up and admitted to the abuse they had endured, even though it was completely against their culture, and there was great risk to them. We were able to minister to them individually and as a group because this barrier had been broken. We watched as they were transformed into strong, confident young women. They came together, committing to support and hold each other accountable. This was a life changing event for them, as they were truly transformed into strong, confident young women.

Through this book, Becky has clearly portrayed step-by-step how to be an overcomer in business, in ministry, and especially in life. You will begin to identify and learn to conquer your personal fears and insecurities that are keeping you from being what God has created you to be. **– Kathy Corbett**, Christ-follower and best friend

Becky has a unique ability to identify spiritual concepts and principles at work in the life of a Christian and the grace to present the right keys of truth and action that will bring freedom to their heart/mind and release them to walk in greater power and influence in the kingdom of God!

I first met Becky 15 years ago when we were a part of a church plant together. Ever since I have known her she has been a lover of truth and passionate to pursue breakthrough in her own life and the lives of others. I can't remember a time when I have talked to Becky and she hasn't referred to her conversations with God as an integral part of her day and the plumb line for her life.

I have seen Becky walk through many hard seasons in her life – yet consistently press into the Lord through prayer and press through the trial by faith. As I have watched her come through these painful circumstances, her life has been marked by greater revelation, greater freedom, and the attainment of new levels of impact and influence in her business and ministry.

I am forever grateful for Becky's friendship and influence on my life. She has spoken things into me and called me up into higher levels of grace more than anyone else in my life. She spoke some things to me early on in my ministry, way ahead of where I was at and my understanding of myself at that time – yet I am now walking in the leadership and identity she foresaw. I always feel strengthened and encouraged to walk in greater fulness of my calling and identity in Christ when I spend time with Becky.

– Anna Latshaw, Executive Director of Hands of Love USA and co-pastor of Dwelling Place Church, Atlanta, accountability partner

4 Phases of Spiritual Warfare:

Navigate Sabotage
Build SUCCESS

Becky Harmon

DEDICATION

To my husband, Jay. Thank you for telling me to just get started writing and not worry about my grammar or how everything was going to work out. You were right; it did.

Thank you, Kathy Corbett, Beverly Lewis, Anna Latshaw, and Verna Law. I am blessed to have covenant friends who have seen me at my worst, kicked me in the butt, and prayed me through.

CONTENTS

ACKNOWLEDGEMENTS

Thank you, Désirée Schroeder, for all you have done to make this professional. It really gave me great comfort to know you were fixing my typos and rearranging what wasn't clear.

Wes, Lauren, Josh, Abby, Will, and Joe: I love you guys and am so thankful for you in my life. All of you have such a great sense of humor and make me laugh so hard with your gifs and stories.

Mom, Brian, Richard, and Ouida: Again, thankful to have such a supportive family. Jay and I have been really blessed by your encouragement.

INTRODUCTION

The moment you decide that you want your life to matter from a kingdom perspective and the Lord to get the glory, you are going to experience spiritual warfare. You're going to receive additional tension if you have a heart to multiply your message through preaching, teaching, coaching, speaking, or writing content that transforms lives for Christ.

Many times, people do not understand as they seek to impact others for the kingdom of God, how much of the revelation and even confidence that God has to give them is related to whether they will make a decision to build an "overcoming identity." In other words, to solve practical problems through prayer and taking bold action. Sometimes it's easier to just go on a mission trip than solve at home what is creating compromise in your life.

I firmly believe in many cases, we are not waiting on God to be "released" into the work of the ministry at a global level, but rather God is waiting for us to push through fear that limits us in our personal leadership. In other words, carrying practical spiritual authority begins in our own identity with Christ, not by doing religious works. It is only then that we can accomplish the mandate of Matthew 28:18-20.

> And Jesus came up and spoke to them, saying, "All authority has been given to Me in heaven and on earth. Go therefore and make disciples of all the nations, baptizing them in the name of the Father and the Son and the Holy Spirit, teaching them to observe all that I have commanded you [...].

Women, not just men, need to be making disciples and being equipped by the church to pray strongly, lead boldly, and multiply their overcoming testimony in others. I believe every Christian should write their own testimony and message of how Christ set them free. If not for ministry purposes, then simply to pass the torch of faith to the next generation.

> And they overcame him by the blood of the Lamb, and by the word of their testimony; and they loved not their lives unto the death. (Revelations 12:11 KJV)

Thus, we come to *why* I wrote this book. In the process of overcoming my challenges (because I had a lot of spiritual bondage when I came to Christ) and equipping and releasing others to overcome their own spiritual warfare, I began to notice what I called *phases* to my clients' spiritual walk that were very similar to the ones I had to move through. I began to take notes years ago on the patterns I saw and to think about this from a strategic perspective as my business was helping people move out of sabotaging patterns and into success. I always have felt the simpler I try to make things to discern and solve for my clients, the faster their identity in Christ is solidified, and the faster they begin to impact others for the kingdom.

This book is absolutely NOT "secret sauce" revelation or levels that are set in stone. The danger in presenting the process that I am describing in this book is that it will be misunderstood as a formula or fast-track to spiritual maturity. I want to be clear that I am not confusing salvation with mental enlightenment. Salvation is free, and we do nothing to earn that. I believe with the Apostle John that there is no private revelation reserved for a few intellectuals and that the body of Christ has received the whole teaching of the power of the cross.

It's just me, as a wife of thirty years, a mother of four adult kids, an identity coach, and a speaker, trying to break things down practically for you so I can help you understand that you are in a battle EVERYDAY if you want to follow God's will for your life, and there are very similar themes that everyone who wants to make an impact will go through. If you have someone break it down simply, you can maybe avoid the pitfalls the enemy has for you and help people receive the truth of God's love for them faster.

The enemy is crafty and wants to take you out before you're empowered to transform others with your own breakthrough. It makes no difference whether you are doing this within your home as a homeschooler, at work as a CEO, or trying to build an impactful business as an entrepreneur or church planter.

It's all the same kind of warfare! You may never want to speak, coach, or share your testimony publicly, but if anything, maybe this book will answer for you why you may be struggling with feeling held back.

The enemy seeks to suppress us through shame and our feelings of poor performance so that we do not share even the smallest of victories we have gained. He whispers in our ears, "You can't lead or disciple anyone; your house is not in enough order!"

In this book, I hope you will recognize how to submit to Christ and the work of the cross in your life daily so that you are able to walk in more joy through your journey. Essentially, I will walk you through four phases of spiritual warfare that I believe every Christian experiences who wants to multiply the message or work God has done in them. It makes no difference whether it is in ministry or a faith-based business like mine where I coach, speak, and consult on how to grow a business practically. I also give you what to watch out for assignment-wise and the identity prayers I give my clients, so you can pray to stand in faith through all your phases.

Here are the phases briefly.

Phase 1 Sabotage: The first assignment is to prevent you from building any spiritual family, support, or relationships that are helping your maturity in Christ.

Phase 2 Sabotage: The second assignment is to cloud your vision, discourage you from pursuing your deepest heart desires, and create barriers between you with God and other people.

Step 3 Sabotage: The third level of spiritual warfare is to prevent you from abiding in the correct spheres of authority and establishing your authority through Christ.

Phase 4 Sabotage: The fourth level of spiritual warfare comes to test your commitment to the call of God on your life, your boldness, and your willingness to pay the price for the freedom of others.

In each chapter, I describe the assignments and how you specifically need to respond in prayer and the corresponding practical leadership application. It has always been a cry of my heart to aim for resurrection, but equally submit with joy to suffering. It's important that we learn to do both, and that prevents us from perverting the message of the Gospel into a prosperity message, one that centers around legalism, or how we are performing at any given time. You cannot walk in authority without learning how to submit to the process and people in your life. I love what Paul said about how we know we are in Christ:

> [F]or we are the true circumcision, who worship in the Spirit of God and glory in Christ Jesus and put no confidence in the flesh (Philippians 3:3).

Now, with that said, I can tell you with all honesty I enjoy the resurrection times in my walk with God a lot more than the dying to self. Hope that wasn't too real for you. I am going to share with you exactly how I applied the Word of God even in the midst of so many wrong decisions and attitudes I had so that you can perceive how great His mercy and patience is with our failures. I want to help you be sent to serve in the kingdom of God through a revelation of His mercy, grace, and love. Jesus never condemns or shames us for being ambitious or failing miserably. He just redirects us by asking, "Do you love me? If so, do this."

Throughout my life, I have read many books on inward meditation, had a handful of practical experiences with God that allowed me to experience the supernatural, and yet at the end of the day, it has always been through suffering that I have gained my greatest breakthroughs. I want to encourage you to not be afraid of restlessness, tribulation, testings, finding out your motives are wrong, or even feeling gut-wrenching emotional pain. It helps us reach out to God for greater dependency and lordship. It becomes fuel for God sending us in His name.

It is my prayer for you that you will become an overcomer in prayer, lead boldly, and learn to multiply your message to set people free for Christ!

Chapter 1
WHERE THE SABOTAGE BEGINS

"Nobody ever defended anything successfully, there is only attack and attack and attack some more."
— General George S. Patton

B efore your salvation, you were no threat to the enemy. However, the moment you confessed Christ as your Lord, you entered an unseen battle.

For our struggle is not against flesh and blood, but against the rulers, against the powers, against the world forces of this darkness, against the spiritual forces of wickedness in the heavenly places. (Ephesians 6:12)

The Father's mission for you? Intentionally share His love and how it set us free, and teach others how to do the same in the name of Jesus.

> Go ye therefore, and teach all nations, baptizing them in the
> name of the Father, and of the Son, and of the Holy Ghost:
> Teaching them to observe all things whatsoever I have
> commanded you: and, lo, I am with you always, even unto
> the end of the world. Amen. (Matthew 28:19-20 KJV)

Satan's mission for you? Create enough fear, trials, temptations, opportunities for offense, worldly distractions, and overt persecution that you not only are rendered ineffective, but your love grows cold. He wants you on survival mode. Endlessly struggling, never experiencing real genuine breakthrough.

Therefore, courage, my friend, is the focus for every decision you make from this point on. There is zero place for passivity in addressing even ordinary obstacles because through overcoming small obstacles, you are building confidence and a testimony that will overcome the enemy.

> [C]asting all your anxiety on Him, because He cares for you.
> Be of sober spirit, be on the alert. Your adversary, the devil,
> prowls around like a roaring lion, seeking someone to
> devour. But resist him, firm in your faith, knowing that the

same experiences of suffering are being accomplished by
your brethren who are in the world. (1 Peter 5:7-9)

This is not about finding a devil under every rock or not
understanding the power of Christ and His grace. It's about facing
the reality behind why you're really struggling with sabotage. Building
the mindsets that lead to a practical execution of faith. The result of
this is a quiet, simple, joy-filled life that is remarkably different than
the world. Authentically and without you having to feel compelled to
drop scripture into every conversation.

Therefore, prepare your minds for action, keep sober in
spirit, fix your hope completely on the grace to be brought
to you at the revelation of Jesus Christ. (1 Peter 1:13)

Now, there are people who will tell you that you are too
intense... "You don't believe there is an actual devil do you?" I have
had a handful of that myself. Along with, "Just stay focused on your
daily gratefulness time, doing good in the world, and go to church on
Sunday."

Now, and I am not trying to offend you right out of the gate, but
typically in my experience these are the same people who rarely
experience lasting victory, influence anyone for the kingdom of God
in their family or at work, or live a passionate, purposeful life.

And here's the thing. I want to walk in a demonstration of
practical power and I hope you do, too. Not the flashy, "BE

3

HEALED" with a slap on the forehead kind of spiritual experience, but being able to really believe from the bottom of your heart that your current obstacle – through prayer, boldness, and God's grace – can be solved.

When this happens consistently, by overcoming your lions and bears, you begin to build a life message that is anointed. Your marriage and family change, the way you serve people in your work changes, and best of all, you will have divine appointments to share with others of how the power of God delivered and transformed your life practically.

This makes sense, right? I bet right now you have a friend who is struggling with family problems, and you might know a faith-filled friend you can send them to that understands and has overcome in that area. The same thing through drugs, alcohol, and financial stress. Essentially, you become a message mentor because you are seeing now through a lens of your obstacles being an opportunity, not a cross to bear. In everything you tackle, you're praying, "Lord Jesus, use this oppression in my life to multiply victory in others."

God has three solutions for anything that is stealing from your joy and sharing an overcoming faith. It's called prayer, worship, and action. Pretty simple. These are the three primary ways He strengthens you so that the message of how His Son delivered you is compelling and anointed!

But the Lord stood by me, and strengthened me; that through me the message might be fully proclaimed, and all the Gentiles might hear: and I was delivered out of the mouth of the lion. (2 Timothy 4:17 ASV)

From the moment you're awake and your feet hit the floor, you have a choice to choose courage or fear. This one focus will make the difference between taking ground for the kingdom or losing it. Decisions that are going to lead to greater peace, so you can serve others or decisions that are going to dilute your faith and boldest identity. How do I know this? I talk to people every day who love God and want to influence for the kingdom in an authentic way, and they can't because they feel double-minded, discouraged, and inconsistent. It's maddening for them. Feeling all the potential and not being able to harness it. It was the same for me.

It would seem easy enough to make right decisions if we believed that God was for us and the difficulty we were experiencing was simply spiritual warfare. But people who have grown up in addictive, shame-based, or legalistic homes really struggle with believing God loves them and will give them breakthrough if they just don't quit. For people that have had emotionally healthy parents or mentors, seeing life through the lens of faith is normal.

For these individuals, overcoming obstacles just requires ownership, an adventurous spirit, and hard work! As a matter of fact, risk is even fun because they don't really struggle with the fear of failure. They have basically learned that people can be counted on to do what they say they will do. They can ask for what they want, and they will be heard and supported if they take ownership of their vision.

On the other hand, if you grew up in a fear-based (idolatrous) home like I did, you perceive much of life through a negative, victimized viewpoint. You are accustomed to working hard for little or no pay-out, and having to strive for affirmation. You're used to people not doing what they say they will do, criticizing your best efforts, hanging you out to dry, and abandoning you when you ask for help. No wonder you feel like you're on survival mode. Ah, you have been, and I know I was.

Honestly, most people are not even aware they have this mindset. This is because they have been under spiritual warfare since they were young children. Passivity, fear, and hiding feels normal to them. They think it's WHO they are identity-wise. They are not the head, they are the tail.

It wasn't until I read the characteristics of an alcoholic home that I realized why receiving a revelation of my identity in Christ and growing my authority took me so many years. It wasn't because I didn't have discipline, enough brains, power, or even consistency. It was because I had the demonic mindset of someone who had grown up with poverty/victimization thinking, even though our family was upper middle class.

It would be helpful for you to read the "13 Characteristics of an Alcoholic Home" by Janet Geringer Woititz, even though your home may not have been addictive. This also applies to shame-based, performance-based, and fear-based homes. If you feel like you have difficulty believing God truly loves you and is for you, please read it thoughtfully and perhaps even ask your closest friends if you have any of these characteristics.

Where My Victimization-Thinking and Sabotages Started

One of my earliest memories of childhood is of my grandfather driving into our neighborhood drunk, yelling my name on a bullhorn as he drove down our street. He thought this was hilarious. I remember the stress it created for my mother, and how she would never leave us alone with him. Another memory was just cleaning my room compulsively. I spent a lot of time in my room as a child because it felt safe to me. Cleaning and isolation became a way for me to process pain.

My father owned Jimmy Bryson's Cocktail Lounge, which was the watering hole for the pilots at Miami International Airport in the 1960s. He slept late on Sundays because it was his only day off. I remember my mom saying when I asked her why Dad didn't go to church with us, "He's tired, he worked late and has to get up early."

This seemed to make a lot of sense to me as a young child. At least until I was eight, and I began to notice he slept face-down on the bed, and nothing could wake him when he was "tired." Completely face down, like you're being smothered to death... but who's checking?

The last memory I have of my father alive was bringing him chicken soup as he recovered in bed with bruises from the top of his head to the bottom of his feet. He had fallen down an entire flight of steel stairs. It was shocking, as he looked like he had been beaten with a baseball bat, and I was thankful that my mother, who had divorced him years earlier, was not there to see it.

I did have God do something remarkable for me two weeks before my father's death that was absolutely supernatural. I had been saved for about eight years at this point and honestly was still struggling with so much bitterness and judgment towards him due to the chaos he constantly brought into our family. My father was very generous financially, but due to his alcoholic patterns there were multiple affairs, fist fights with customers, and outbursts of anger at home. We just never really knew what to expect on any given day. He could be on the floor passed out or working out in the yard in an okay mood. It felt I was always walking on egg shells.

My dad was well respected in our community because of his generosity but he did not give out any affirmation. This meant even as a married mother of four at age 30, if I pleased him, Jay and I would randomly receive $500.00 in the mail in cash for a simple holiday like Valentine's Day. If I set a boundary he didn't like, in a drunken stupor he would cut up pictures of him and me together, mail them to me, and cut me off for a couple of months. It was painful, and I was in counseling in my 20s for years to try and build boundaries that helped me recover. My youngest, Joe, was only almost two at the time when I received a phone call from my mother that my dad had fallen.

That night, I had a dream. In it, there was a flood, and my dad was sleeping in the house, but I could not wake him to get him out. I shouted, screamed, and watched the water rise up to his bed and over his body. I had to swim out of the house and leave him or I would have drowned myself. When I awoke, I grabbed my Bible and asked the Lord what the dream was about. He gave me a scripture of flood waters rising (told me to turn to the exact scripture that described my dream, although I had no previous knowledge of it) and impressed on me strongly that he would die within a week. He told me point blank to fly down to Miami and let go of the bitterness I had in my heart towards him.

I booked a flight the next day to go down to Miami and spend time with him. I called my brother Brian, who was newly married at the time, and my half-brother Jim, who was a doctor, and told them that I was concerned Dad would die. Jim told me he had seen the X-rays, and it was not life threatening. I did not want to tell him that I had a God-dream and that's why I flew down quickly because I didn't want him to think I was crazy, but I did tell my brother Brian about the dream. Both of them told me they thought Dad would be fine. He died that week, and the grace was I had an opportunity to tell my father I forgave him, repent for my bitterness, and receive closure before he passed. It was also the beginning for me of learning how to hear God during crisis and act even if no one else was.

My mother was a faithful woman and safe place for me when I was growing up. She kept the house clean, cooked great meals, ironed Dad's clothes, and then worked to put me through college. This was despite the fact both her parents were alcoholics, she was moved from home to home in her teenage years, had nothing but a high school diploma, and married an alcoholic herself. She took us to church every Sunday, even though my father would not accompany her, so we were exposed to the faith.

But, even though I attended the services, the truth was, I was not a friend of God. I was much too angry to be God's friend. So rather than actually listen while I was there, I drew pictures on the back of the tithe envelopes during the preaching.

When it was my turn to serve as an "altar girl," I burned the ceiling panels as I waited to walk down the aisle with my "white robes" (I have no idea how I didn't burn down the church). Suffice it to say, I was a handful growing up. I genuinely know why animals in the wild eat their young. I was constantly getting into trouble in any group I joined. This made it difficult for my mother to actually ever let down emotionally because it was only a matter of time before she would get a phone call saying, "MaryAnn, come pick up your daughter."

Here are just some of the actual calls she received:

"Becky got in a fight at school and is demanding to be withdrawn."

"Becky got lost in Disney World because she didn't listen to directions, and the park shut down before they could find her."

"Becky fell down a flight of stairs because she was climbing them in roller skates."

"Becky had to be taken to the hospital because she faked broken ribs to get out of finishing Girl Scout camp."

"Becky needs to be taken for X-rays because she broke three toes from running around camp without her sneakers on, despite being told multiple times to put them back on."

"Becky needs to be picked up from counseling because she told the counselor to go %#$&@* himself, that she didn't have any psychological issues."

When I threatened to run away at the age of 16, my mom walked calmly to my room, pulled out my drawers, and began to stuff my clothes in my suitcase to make it easier to leave. It wasn't until this point in my adolescence that I thought... *Hmmm. That is not a normal motherly response, I think she is serious. I probably should just keep my mouth shut and quit acting out.*

When I went away to Florida State University for college, I am sure she wept simply for the respite of peace she was going to get from me leaving the house.

To compound my rebellious personality, I was firstborn and extremely performance-driven. I had voices screaming at me internally 24 hours a day that made me measure everything I did and everyone around me. It was sheer torment.

On some days, the voices of disappointment and expectations were so loud I contemplated suicide. I was already occasionally blacking out from alcohol binges and only graduated because I made a little pact with myself that I would get my papers written before I started partying Thursday through Saturday. Sunday was spent with me hungover.

By the grace of God, I met Christ in college through some covert, ninja stalking, chocolate-chip-enticing, Jesus grandmas. They were stealthy in their approach and set me up for the evangelistic close quite nicely.

I was doing an internship for Criminology with a program called Outward Bound. Of course, it wasn't a stretch for me to do an internship there because I was a juvenile delinquent at this point in my life. On Wednesday nights after the teens went to bed, we would play cards and eat cookies, or so that's what I thought was happening.

Little did I know, they were praying for my salvation. Night after night, they brought me cookies and asked me questions like... "So, tell us about your engagement."

I would share in detail all our exciting upcoming plans. And then slowly, the question line turned to this:

Cookie-toting evangelistic ninja: "So, you are assured of your salvation (big warm smile). So, tell us, how do you KNOW exactly?"

Becky: "Oh, well, I went to church every Sunday and was confirmed in the Methodist Church." I continued with all the nice things I did for the senior citizens and how many Girl Scout cookies I sold, just so she knew beyond a shadow of a doubt that I wasn't going to hell in a handbag.

Cookie-toting evangelistic ninja: "So, have you ever stolen a pencil? Taken the Lord's name in vain? Dishonored your parents? Have you had sex with your fiancé before your marriage?"

I was sweating bullets...visualizing all the quarters I stole out of my dad's coin bank on his dresser, the FIVE BILLION lies I had told since I was old enough to speak, and I was living with my fiancé Jim... And what? I got no points for working with the senior citizens? This was outrageous!

She stopped and let it all just sink in because she was a professional.

I went to bed tormented with my own performance-based world rocked. The next day, she invited me to Wednesday night service. I wasn't quite sure why everyone was raising their hands during the music as it seemed rather rude to interrupt the band with questions. (I had never seen anyone raise their hands during singing so I had no idea what was happening.)

I made a mental note of where the doors were located so I could escape quickly if needed, as I was quite sure these women were part of a cult. I sat down to listen to the pastor share his message, and slowly, I began to feel uncomfortable and aware of a void in my life that partying couldn't fill. I felt empty and I was scared of hell. I know not everyone is scared into salvation, but I can tell you I feared the fact that someone had clearly explained to me the consequences of not choosing life through Christ, or choosing my own way of doing things. I was afraid if I died I would go to hell. I wrestled during the whole service with fearing hell and yet not wanting to give up my worldly lifestyle. There was a raging battle in my mind and heart over who was going to be Lord over my life: Christ or myself.

I thought to myself, "As soon as I become a Christian, I have to change my ways." I had no understanding of just stepping out in faith and accepting the work Christ had done for me. I knew He died for my sins, but I still thought I would have to have the will power to change, and I was terrified because I knew I would fail. I went back and forth in my mind, back and forth with increasing conviction that I could die tonight and not really have peace that I would go to heaven. Finally, I broke down sobbing because the revelation hit me. "I can't do it. I try and live purposefully, and I fail constantly. I don't feel significant, I sabotage myself constantly. I don't know God, even though I want to live a purposeful life. I need help. I receive you, Lord Jesus."

The two evangelistic ninjas were beside me, and I was baptized in the Holy Ghost and started speaking in tongues. Which was a problem immediately because I had been confirmed Methodist and I didn't believe in tongues and associated it with snake-handling crazy people. Now, I was apparently part of the snake-wrangling team without even signing up for it. Methodists were dignified, which was how I perceived truly spiritual people. For example: People who are spiritual look like Catholic nuns. They have a bonnet, long skirt, and wear a big Jesus cross necklace. They help poor people.

Also, I had a spiritual gift that I had no knowledge on how to use, and the spiritual warfare started immediately. I came home from the church and shared Jesus with the kids. I prayed for one of the campers, and she chose to run off grounds that night. They fired the two women and myself, and I had to redo a whole extra internship. Because of this, I lost touch with them and received no follow-up discipleship.

I was really messed up emotionally, and I believe to this day due to a couple of situations I had happen that I was demonically oppressed. I had a seriously judgmental attitude, didn't trust God, and definitely didn't trust people. I really struggled with authority figures, had no filter when speaking to them, and expected to be disappointed. I thought like a victim though I carried myself externally like everything was successful and great. I had no ability to grasp God's kindness and patience, no understanding of my identity in Christ or the authority that accompanied it, and zero ability to walk in the spirit long enough to overcome obstacles.

I didn't understand I had to grow into a Christlike identity. And now, here's the thing, and I hope you hear my heart on this if you have been let down by organized churches, Christian leaders that didn't walk their talk, or otherwise you just haven't had a great experience with the local church. This is much of the reason you need to recognize that spiritual warfare will come to you especially inside the church. This shouldn't be offensive to you. The church is made of different people in various stages of their faith. Expect it from people that you think should know better. If you believe you have a call to ministry on your life, God will absolutely orchestrate offense from a ministry perspective to refine and test you. This is why it's important for you to have one or two spiritual mothers and fathers watching over you that you can learn how to respond by. Fail these tests and leave the church, and you might as well just quit on Jesus because HE DIED FOR THE CHURCH. You're going to want to have people who know your heart and can remind you of who you are identity-wise when misunderstanding and rejection come your way.

And here's the next newsflash for you: If you grew up in a dysfunctional family, you will have tons of idolatry coming against you CONSTANTLY and you will have to pull it down to keep moving forward successfully. I love this scripture because it indicates that growth comes in stages for everyone and is related to just being a good spiritual mom or dad, not just professional theologians:

> I write to you, little children, because your sins are forgiven you for His name's sake. I write to you fathers, because ye have known Him that is from the beginning. I write unto you, young men, because ye have overcome the wicked one. I write to you, little children, because ye have known the Father. I have written to you, fathers, because ye have known Him that is from the beginning. I have written to you, young men, because ye are strong, and the word of God abideth in you, and ye have overcome the wicked one. (1 John 2:12-14 KJV)

Here's what I want you to know at the beginning of reading this book. It's important to ask yourself if you are progressing to new levels of spiritual growth. Because if you feel "stuck," disconnected, or frustrated with perpetual cycles you can't break out of, you're most likely under spiritual warfare already.

You have tension coming to you because you want to live purposely and make a difference with your life. Now for some of you, this might be the first time you have ever had anyone tell you, "Hey, you're not crazy. You're not rebellious. You just haven't had any training on your identity or been mentored on how to move through the levels of growth FASTER than you can do it alone."

So, even though salvation and your identity in Christ is INSTANT, the process of learning how to break through negative patterns and walk in authority is going to take time to learn.

You move to more influence, more authority, and promotion by learning how trust the Lord, obey Christ, and love people in word and deed.

If you have prayed this prayer one time: "Help me live a purposed, significant life," then you have drawn a line in the sand. Essentially you have decided to live intentionally. The enemy does not like you becoming strategic about anything. And it doesn't matter if you whispered this prayer in your prayer closet, or you prayed it at the altar after a convicting message. You said it. And now the enemy knows you who you are, and his aim is to take you out. Why? Because passionate people win more often than the apathetic people. Especially in a war. Now, whether or not you feel like you are doing a great job at that right now is not the issue. You may be saying, "But Becky, I am no threat to Satan because I can't even make it church on most Sundays or avoid cussing at my children. I fall asleep praying, and frankly, I disappoint myself. I can't even stay consistent and lose the 30 pounds I've been wanting to ditch for ten years. I'm in a marriage that stinks, and I'm exhausted trying to make it work."

The problem for the devil is that you desire to change. All issues in the kingdom revolve around the heart, whether for positive change or negative backsliding. Begin now to write out this scripture card and confess it over yourself daily. I will be giving you twelve more in order to help you solidify your identity. Through these, you will learn to be an overcomer in prayer, lead boldly, and multiply your testimony with grace.

Your Identity Work and Confession

Father, thank You for illuminating me to the fact that despite the spiritual warfare I am receiving, I AM called to go into all the world and preach the gospel to all creation. Your Word says this about my purpose today…these signs will accompany those who believe: In the name of Jesus they will cast out demons, they will speak with new tongues! I will not go into exile from a lack of knowledge; I will not be famished, I will not be thirsty! (Isaiah 5:13) I will be like a tree planted by water that extends its roots so when the heat is applied to my life, I will have no fear. My leaves will be green in my spirit, and even when others are experiencing a drought of provision and hearing from you, I will flourish. (Jeremiah 17:8) I AM willing to have your identity, Lord, as a messenger.

Chapter 2
THE FIGHT BEGINS

"Being ready is not what matters. What matters is winning after you get there."
— Lt. Gen. Victor H. Krulak, USMC, April 1965

Your old identity comes with a lot of strong feelings that, frankly, you're going to have to learn to take before the Lord and examine before you follow them. Some of the resistance you may feel reading this book absolutely will be the enemy.

You may have painful emotions arise as this content triggers memories or offenses you may have repressed or forgotten. You may possibly have idolatry in place in your heart that has been in your family for generations. I am telling you this at the beginning of the book because I have seen people quit during coaching because they underestimated the amount of spiritual warfare they were going to get from overcoming their obstacles. Tension is NORMAL in the kingdom of God.

Lordship and following Jesus will CONFRONT the places in your life where you have compromised, hid, and otherwise not received accountability for. Receiving discipline correctly is what makes us true sons and daughters. If you are without mentoring in your life, you are wandering spiritually. People who wander off during war are captured by the enemy. That's a strong statement but it's accurate.

Everyone, EVERYONE needs people in their life pouring into them, guiding, and guarding them. Receiving mentoring begins with a heart attitude of humility. It involves being open to pray about thought processes that make you uncomfortable, checking them with the scripture, thinking for yourself, but yet seeking to be unified with your brothers and sisters in Christ.

If you have questions about the content or scriptures, just circle the parts you disagree with or don't understand. Keep reading. Talk about them with an older, more experienced mentor in the faith. Keep reading. FINISH the book! Your deliverance and mind will be renewed as you keep moving forward. If you couple the content with confessing the declarations and scriptures I provide, you will receive faster breakthrough if you feel resistance.

The quicker you view your identity and your DESTINY through a lens of actual military engagement with an objective of ADVANCING TO WIN, the more successful you will be at pushing through all adversity in your life.

Practice the I AM confessions in every chapter. Speak them out loud daily and to the spirit realm around you. Just because you can't touch or see it doesn't mean it's not directing you. You may have to do this 50 times a day. I have had people carry index cards around with them in their pocket or purse before they could memorize them. Don't be surprised at what begins to happen to you from day one of reading this book if you follow my instructions exactly.

Let's review: I want you to put the scripture I give you below on an index card and memorize it if you fit into any of the following categories:

1.   You are a new Christian and you do not have someone mentoring or watching over you, spiritually keeping you accountable for what you say you want to grow in.

2.   You have had a bad experience with leadership in your past church and you haven't found a church body you enjoy.

3.   You are visiting churches, trying to find where you fit in but haven't officially joined yet.

4.   You can't seem to build stability emotionally. It's up one day, down the next. You're exhausted with trying to fix yourself and feeling hopeless.

When I pray, I always take time to do confessions out of the Word of God, as it solidifies my identity in Christ. I want you to win the battle of your faith and see your vision established on the earth.

Sometimes when people hear the word discipline, or spiritual fathering, mothering, or mentoring, they get this feeling of, "Hey, that's not my identity. That's my neighbor John, or Lisa, or my pastor! He or she has talent, intellect and charisma! I'm great at being inconsistent. I could never overcome the current obstacles I have right now. I will never be a leader of others, let alone lead myself well. I deserve to struggle because I make wrong decisions constantly."

Here's the bottom line. Your failure and poverty of spirit leaves a door open for God to be glorified. So, if you have never been part of a spiritual family and have not had access to leaders pouring into you, be encouraged! A matter of fact, sometimes God chooses those of us who have wandered away just because when we gain success, it so encourages other people to be brave! He gets more glory!

You may have already got that in place like I did, so know we can move to the success part AND guess what? The Holy Spirit is called the Comforter, the Spirit of Truth. He's not measuring you because that would be the complete opposite of the agenda of the mission of Christ who followed everything His Father did. Once you accept Him into your heart, He is not judging! He is praying for you and asking you to return to loving Him wholeheartedly! When you fail, He doesn't criticize, shame us, or remind us of how we could've done a better job. He just asks us one thing: "Do you love Me?" And He gives us the one directive we need to regain our boldness!

So when they had finished breakfast, Jesus said to Simon Peter, "Simon, son of John, do you love Me more than these?" He said to Him, "Yes, Lord; You know that I love You." He said to him, "Tend My lambs." He said to him again a second time, "Simon, son of John, do you love Me?" He said to Him, "Yes, Lord; You know that I love You." He said to him, "Shepherd My sheep." He said to him the third time, "Simon, son of John, do you love Me?" Peter was grieved because He said to him the third time, "Do you love Me?" And he said to Him, "Lord, You know all things; You know that I love You." Jesus said to him, "Tend My sheep." (John 21:15-17)

[B]ut I have prayed for you, that your faith may not fail; and you, when once you have turned again, strengthen your brothers." (Luke 22:32)

When we accept Christ into our hearts, we receive access to redemptive forgiveness, patience, comfort, and hope, because that's what the kingdom of God is! The Father, Son and Holy Ghost exist to illuminate you to the will of God for your life, reveal to you how to pray, and empower you to be the overcomer you have always dreamed of being. You can also be absolutely assured of your salvation without worrying if you don't "do Christianity" correctly you're going to hell.

Most of the time, when we become anxious it's because we have not recognized how to yield and follow Christ. I know that took me a long time to learn. One of the quickest ways we can grow in our coachability from God is to recognize boundaries that keep our heart peaceful. The Holy Spirit will actually help us obey Christ who IS the

Word of God. The Father, Son and Holy Ghost all agree. Think of scripture as a boundary. A boundary is Christ. Christ is life incarnate. So, when you speak the Word of God, you are speaking LIGHT into the atmosphere and even if it's chaotic, you are calling it into order. Now it may take time to appear orderly, but by faith and by your work, you will bring it into order.

For example:

In the beginning was the Word, and the Word was with God, and the Word was God. The same was in the beginning with God. All things were made by him; and without him was not any thing made that was made. In him was life; and the life was the light of men. And the light shineth in darkness; and the darkness comprehended it not. (John 1:1-5 KJV)

Now, think about these scriptures:

And God said out loud (and if God and Jesus modeled that, let's COPY THAT!):

The earth was formless and void, and darkness was over the surface of the deep, and the Spirit of God was moving over the surface of the waters. Then God said, "Let there be light"; and there was light. (Genesis 1:2-3)

If you had donated something worth millions of dollars to a museum, they would put it under glass and maybe even put a guard there so all the kids coming through didn't put their grimy fingerprints on it. That would be a reasonable request, right?

Normal is to GUARD what we value and to ask other people to respect that value. People who aren't trying to take advantage of you will respect your boundaries. People who are healthy and successful know good boundaries are part of great leadership. Consequently, people who are out for themselves or just aren't living significant lives will be offended by the fact that you value yourself, your time, and your purpose, and even try to make you compromise on your boundaries. Why? Because they either don't value themselves enough to do the same or they are trying to manipulate you for their own means.

When you come into contact with someone who is guilt-tripping you to make the decision they want you to make or not listening to you communicate heart boundaries, you are now under spiritual warfare. If you don't assert your authority in Christ the correct way, you will be conformed to their agenda rather than God's. This is how nice people get sucked into cults and organizations that shame them for leaving, suck them dry financially, or worse, threaten them physically.

In our childhoods we were supposed to be affirmed, valued, and allowed to enjoy our childhoods without having to perform for love. If one of your parents or both were fear-based, shame-based or addiction-based, most likely you grew up not knowing your value or having to do whatever necessary to survive emotionally and feel loved. There are tons of churches today that pretty much center their message around performance-based thinking. This is because a lot of people who go into ministry are actually from these kind of survival-based homes. These churches are easy to discern because their message is focused on you doing things properly to please God rather than centering you on the accomplished work of Christ.

People who are on survival mode don't do any vision casting. They are just trying to get their basic needs met and set up dictatorships that promote their agenda.

So, whether you realize it or not, you could be unconsciously attracted towards relationships, jobs, and even churches that are legalistic, controlling, and even frown upon growing you in leadership because your growth minimizes their authority. I know it sounds crazy, but if you have experienced it, you know how easily this happens.

All it takes to begin to move through spiritual warfare is a willingness to learn the Word of God, speak it consistently, and then stick to your vision long enough to see it come to pass. When you do this, you begin to gain confidence and you become a respected person because people understand who you are identity-wise. We teach people HOW to respect us by our clarity, our consistency and our unwillingness to compromise on our personal leadership. This occurs in every area of your life: your faith, your finances, your parenting, your job, and the list goes on and on.

Again, think strategically about actual military warfare to win. When you decided to follow Jesus, you joined the spiritual Marines. You didn't sign up for the Boy Scouts or Girl Scouts. This is a big difference in mindset on how you approach obstacles based on if you're tackling them to earn a badge and get approval from people or you're there to take territory and take out the enemy, PERIOD.

Christianity is a forward-advancing, hard-hitting team mission, but instead of an M-16, you're carrying the Word of God. The Word of God will create a BOLD IDENTITY and break every bondage you are currently experiencing if you work with God to co-create a life you love. It's my heart to see you equipped to be an overcomer and then use your experiences to help other people receive Christ. Let's end today with a confession of WHO you are!

Your Identity Work and Confession

I AM the temple of the Holy Spirit. I AM not my own. I AM bought with the blood of Christ, and therefore today I will glorify God with my body (1 Corinthians 6:19-20). My transgressions have been wiped out like a thick cloud, and I have been redeemed from my past. I will not look back but instead I will be future-focused on reaching people with the mercy of Christ (Isaiah 44:22). I will watch over myself and the entire flock of friends and family I have as an overseer. I AM a shepherd of souls (Acts 20:28). Today I AM being placed into a spiritual family and being brought out of the chains that have held me captive because I AM a follower of Christ (Psalm 68), yielded to

His plans for my life. I AM obeying the promptings of the Holy Spirit when it is revealed to me and choosing to lay my life down for others rather than do my own thing.

Chapter 3
FRONTAL ASSAULTS HAPPEN THROUGH TEAMS

"The Marine Corps is your family, too. You may not have a mother here, but you have a [...] pile of fathers, uncles, and brothers."
– Bud Rudesill

S atan's long-term mission is to prevent you from the following: 1) Knowing the love of Christ; 2) Being set in the body of Christ in your boldest identity zone (practical and spiritual gifting), so you can be... 3) Sharing Christ resurrected with others.

You can want to serve Jesus all you want, but until you reach the place you're willing for Him to become Lord of your isolationist idolatry, you're not in it to win.

So how do you recognize if you're in Phase 1 and need a revelation of teaming? This is not an exhaustive list, but here are some of the statements my clients have communicated that let me know they are hitting Phase 1 and the Lord is asking them to overcome independence and be prepared to be set into the body correctly.

"No one really likes me. They just feel bad for me. They know I am a real mess."

"I'm just lazy. I know what to do but I just don't do it."

"It's only a matter of time before my spouse finds a more attractive or smarter person and leaves me."

"I am not a 'people' person. I don't do teams, groups or organizational church."

"If I share how I really feel, I will be minimized or told that's silly I shouldn't feel that way."

"If I act on what I believe God is saying to me, people will tell me I am not hearing God."

"People may not say anything negative to my face, but they are going to talk about me being rebellious or prideful when I leave the room."

"I don't have any real call of God on my life because I never receive any big prophetic words on anything great I will do."

"If I set that boundary or say 'no,' people are going to think I am not a servant."

"My time is not as valuable as other people's requests. It's selfish to take time every day for myself."

"Nobody will ever listen to me. What do I have to say that 1,000 other people haven't said better. I should follow and not try and lead anything."

"I wish I had Susie's personality. She is more like Jesus than I am."

I know when I was engaging in Phase 1, I heard all day long the most hurtful messages in my head and heart: "There is no big purpose in life for you. People don't like you. You're hard to get along with. Quit bothering God with your double-minded prayers; He is listening to other people that are sold out for Him. If you were in the will of God, life would be easier for you, and you would have more friends. You, my friend, are the last-picked person for the team, and frankly, no one really wanted you in anyway."

You know what is really going on spiritually if you're struggling with these statements inwardly?

This is an unchallenged assignment of rejection meant to keep you from being set in the body correctly. And if you don't deal with it HEAD ON, it will prevent you from building true spiritual family and covenant relationships, because you are resisting becoming unified to a greater degree. You will wait to feel like you fit in, and even though you have access to fathers and mothers in the faith, aunts and uncles, sisters and brothers... you don't do the work to align yourself for it. You hold back from asking for input. You wait to become involved in activities that the group is investing in. You wait to be asked. You wait and wait. Why? Because the devil is constantly reminding you of past relational failures, telling how risky, embarrassing and limiting it will be for you if you let down the shields and trust. People might think you're stand-offish but really, you're just struggling with trusting that people are going to be faithful to you.

So, what I am describing to you is an actual demonic assignment to keep you from being released into your ministry gifting and growing a mindset of community, unity, and spiritual family. But here's the thing you need to recognize: God is actually giving you an opportunity to go through HIS boot camp.

Everyone who grows in their identity has had to go through this very phase that you now find yourself in, and they have passed this test, and you can, too.

Let me explain it to you this way. You want to know why when you're a Marine, you're a Marine for life? It's because once you go through their grueling boot camp and you don't quit, you're forever changed. It's a process that earns you respect. You have essentially chosen to sign up for a lifestyle that will define your identity inter-generationally.

This is why God gives you the opportunity to go through His processes of emotional misunderstanding and outright REJECTION. It's because it makes you RISE up and have to take ownership of your own spiritual gifting and the power you're going to walk in.

In a society filled with disposable relationships, this kind of commitment is risky because it requires you to commit to more emotional transparency. It challenges during every confrontation whether you will think of Christ and His love for others or you will preserve "self." See you can't be placed in the body to function correctly until God knows you're going to be a safe leader.

Safe leaders are always thinking of protecting other people's hearts first and they attract covenant relationships. They have insight that their ability to love and be mission-minded is no longer about them. Through this crucible, you move out of survival thinking into the next phase of influence and take even more ground from the enemy.

In leadership there is a concept called the "Rule of 5." This thought process was made famous by Jim Rohn, who said that we are all, identity-wise, a combination of the five people we spend the most time with. Do you want to know why in the military you eat together, study together, physically train together, go to chapel together, shower, poop, and get shamed together for not taking enough ownership?

They have 13 weeks to take you from a whiny, selfish, entitled child to a lean, mean, mature fighting team. This self-discipline and TEAMING actually delivers you from potential death from sabotaging yourself in battle-like conditions.

It causes you to think and act in unity under immense pressure and hardship with no thought to your own personal safety. It's all about the mission. The group transparency literally peels away your personal sense of privacy and what you consider your dignity to be about. In the Marines, as in the apostolic early church, personal respect should be tied to how courageously we act to lay down our life for others.

Instead of growing up in this kind of culture, here's what has happened instead for many people. They grew up with enabling (people who listen to them whine without challenging them to become a greater leader by instituting boundaries), performance-based, or angry people in their inner circle, and because this is FAMILIAR (comfortable) to them, they gravitate to individuals who are too selfish and prideful for sacrificial service or any kind of personal accountability.

Independent people typically make fear-based decisions that keep them from receiving God's best for their life. They are loners. Why? Because emotional survival is what is "normal" relationally to them! However, this is what you need to know in order to begin to be integrated into God's kingdom at a successful level and get passed Phase 1.

If you don't have anyone you are meeting with routinely for accountability that will ask you hard questions or pray with you about what is challenging you, you're stuck in Phase 1.

If you are in pain emotionally and aren't asking for support, you're stuck in Phase 1 whether you are a CEO, pastor, or a college student.

If you feel stressed in groups of people, you are stuck in Phase 1 if you allow it to prevent you from operating in a team or serving in groups.

If you feel huge potential to love and be loved but deep down didn't feel like stability is for you, you are stuck in Phase 1.

If you don't learn how to work with teams, you will never be given a revelation of your spiritual calling and placement in the body of Christ.

So, I want you to know if you're experiencing this right now, this is ACTUAL SPIRITUAL WARFARE to prevent you from building relationships that will make you an OVERCOMER. This kind of spiritual warfare will make you literally feel crazy – as in serious psychiatric problems, panic attacks, socialization problems, addictions, and compulsive behaviors.

You're not broken beyond repair. You don't need a decade of therapy or anti-depressants. You need faith, to know the power of God through identity work, and to get past Phase 1 so you begin to experience the power of God's love through spiritual family. You do this by doing the work I have described to you in the last chapter and being willing to increase lordship into your life. Lordship does not come without you trusting to open yourself up for mentoring.

Aristotle defined the word "community" as a group established by men/women having shared values. Something powerful happens when you choose to become part of a unified group vision and begin to open your heart to build community. Biblical covenant even is much deeper and more transformational than just a community that

Aristotle experienced. When someone decided to enter in to a covenant relationship with another person, it was for their entire lives. It had personal implications as well as financial applications.

This is one of the reasons why in the early church there was great power. Sacrificial covenant relationships had been modeled to the disciples personally by Jesus, and this was a revelation the apostles were imparting daily as people were converted. The apostles were called to not just be messengers of God's grace and forgiveness, but of His supernatural, sacrificial power. This was a revelation that was matched with daily actions in small communities.

They were people like you and me, meeting in people's houses and at synagogues, eating, drinking, praying, and fasting together for a manifest power of God upon everyone's lives. There was an expectation that when new converts confessed Christ, they were willing to subject themselves to the discipline of the whole community for the common purpose of the kingdom being expanded into their community in a greater way. There was a LIFESTYLE of teaming that would turn the world upside down. They were willing to be sanctified, separated, and consecrated in every area of their lives.

When you experience covenant friendships, unity, and the power of prayer that flows out of these relationships, it will supersede anything natural you will find in clubs, organizations, sororities, or even your own family if they are not followers of Christ. When you understand your identity in Christ and covenant relationships, you do not need to appeal to people to do the right thing racially, politically, or financially. Covenant relationships give you an empathy for your mother, father, brother, and sister in need – locally and globally. And this is what the church is called to exemplify. So, it makes no difference as to how spiritual you feel, if you are not part of a spiritual team or church with a mission focus, you are operating alone and are in danger of being picked off by the enemy.

Covenant relationships used to be sealed by ceremony. It's when promises are released, and blessings are established inter-generationally. When God entered into a convenient with Abraham, He changed his name, promising him that his seed would be as numerous as the stars of the heavens. He had Abraham arrange sacrificed animals, and when He put him to sleep, He walked through the middle of it as a smoking fire pot to symbolize that there was NOTHING Abraham could do to make it come to pass. It was all on God (Genesis 15).

This also foreshadowed Christ and how we cannot do anything to earn our righteous identity and the promises that come forth from that.

In 1 Samuel 18, there is a covenant relationship described between David and Jonathan, Saul's son. The Bible says from the moment David stopped speaking to Saul, Jonathan loved him as his own soul. Jonathan stripped off his own robe, and they exchanged weapons pledging themselves to each other's defense. What's important to note is that this spiritual relationship even superseded the blood relationship Jonathan had with his father, Saul, and extended kindness and financial provision to Jonathan's sons!

This understanding of covenant relationships went deep in all the disciples. The Last Supper that Jesus had with His covenant friends, before He was crucified, created a focus for them to begin their lives as messengers with. It was also a "ceremony" that began to help establish new covenant thinking.

Now, I want to cover some very simple basics and I would like you to think about this from the perspective that you have been following Jesus as one of His disciples for three years. You left home and possibly your business to travel with Him. Jesus was not a theology lesson to you; He mentored you personally.

You laughed with Him. You slept on the ground with your team members and Him. You saw Him deliver insane people into a right mind and heal people with leprosy with a simple touch. You saw Him walk through a crowd of religious teachers who were frothing at the mouth when He overturned their tables and wanted to kill Him. You have seen things that have deeply, passionately impacted you. And now He is telling you that He is not going to be establishing a political system on earth, but instead He's leaving to make you a home, so you and Him can be together eternally. Also, He has some things He wants you to do so you can live a life of leadership that will change others before you get there.

He wants you to understand living in covenant with Him and your new relationships. That you will serve each other humbly and sacrificially despite disputes, if at all possible, staying in unity for the mission's sake. Jesus did this first before He embraced the cross by washing the feet of the disciples to share with them the value of humility and self-sacrifice. "No longer do I call you servants, […] but I have called you friends […]" (John 15:15 NKJV). You cannot have covenant without sacrificing deeply, authentically, and painfully for your family and covenant community. In other words, you cannot have covenant alone with just you, Jesus, and your knowledge of the Bible.

Next, He prayed for them that the Father would not take them out of suffering and the world, but that they would be overcomers of evil, and that their identities would not be diluted from it. That they would be in ONE in unity, and that because of this, the world would know Christ and that they had been sent by HIM.

Covenant relationships do life together. This is why we are told in Hebrews 10:25 to not forsake the assembling of the saints, and why watching church on the internet will not be enough LIFE for you relationally. You cannot take communion online.

Taking communion in remembrance of the Last Supper, in addition to eating and drinking together in order to build relationally, helps overcome offenses and enjoy the benefits of your spiritual family. Early Christians ate together daily and later weekly with each participant bringing food, and with the meal eaten in a common room. The Moravians and other denominations practice this still today calling this a love feast.

Covenant relationships are built and reflected in baptism within a body of believers. When you receive Christ into your heart, water baptism in the body of believers you will be accountable to helps announce to the world and to your spiritual family that you have decided to leave behind your old identity and are willing to be discipled and grow in your identity in Christ. Christ modeled water baptism by John, and it was an apostolic teaching that we still encourage today.

Hopefully, you can see that this isn't a set of religious rules or regulations, and this is why Satan fights so hard to prevent you from becoming established in covenant relationships within your local church and leadership teams. Covenant comes out of the local assembly and teams, and it's where you can receive teaching, build real accountability, and have prayer and fellowship.

If you have not had positive experiences with authority figures or groups, you will stay STUCK at this first level of influence until you learn how to forgive yourself and the people who have hurt you this far in life.

You will struggle with feeling insignificant to God and others. This attack leads to much double-mindedness, anger, and insecurity. Why? Because you're still stuck in an old identity and haven't chosen to trust God and do the work! This is also why many people spiritually wander in the body of Christ and never seem to get breakthrough.

You have to choose to confess the Word of God daily. You have to choose to not forsake the assembly of the saints. You have to choose to pray when you feel discouraged. You have to choose to forgive when you're offended or have been treated unjustly. You have to choose to humble yourself before mentors in the faith and follow what they suggest if they have been successful and you can see the fruit of their lives.

Let me be clear. Satan wants to wear you out emotionally with victimization-thinking before a righteous indignation rises up in you. Yes! Get angry at the devil for making you feel like you take one step forward and two steps back! Get mad at him that you can't seem to find your place! Get mad that you don't feel a camaraderie with other Christians, a significance, and you're not living an epic life of faith! Get mad and then start doing the work to become a force to be reckoned with!

Right from the beginning, your Father desired for you to be part of a team. To experience a camaraderie with other Christians, to walk in significance, and live an epic life of faith pursuing a vision that glorifies God.

Let's review as we move into the next chapter. The original team is the Father, the Son and the Holy Ghost. Three in one. Distinct and different roles, but one God. This triune team was the first spiritual family. Spiritual family is an important concept, because without it, you can never live a life full of purpose and spiritual impact. When you understand and are knit into a spiritual team, it accelerates your identity being formed. Or conversely, without it, you struggle with doubt, unbelief, and poor decision making.

This is because teaming was and still is in the heart of our Father. It was taking place in the heavenly realm even before creation. He loves big spiritual families (His people throughout the world) but really, He loves just two or three people working together in unity. It's a human perspective to think that one thousand men would be more powerful than two men. But what the Word of God says is the power of unity and agreement turns two who agree in prayer into a thousand, because God is in the midst of you through the Holy Spirit. If you cannot work within a team environment, in unity, you cannot be like Jesus.

Your Identity Work and Confession

Scriptures for your index cards:

See, how good and how pleasing it is for brothers to live together as one! It is like oil of great worth poured on the head, flowing down through the hair on the face, even the face of Aaron, and flowing down to his coat. It is like the morning water of Hermon coming down upon the hills of Zion. For there the Lord has given the gift of life that lasts forever. (Psalm 133:1-3 NLV)

I AM being positioned this week to be sent as a blessing to new friends, new covenant relationships, and a loving spiritual family! I trust God that He is knitting me into a body where I can be a blessing and I will not come under a spirit of rejection and isolation.

"This is My commandment, that you love and unselfishly seek the best for one another, just as I have loved you. No one has greater love than to lay down his life for his friends. You are My friends if you keep on doing what I command you." (John 15:12-14 AMP)

I AM going to look for an opportunity today to lay down my life for someone else in my family and community. I will stop thinking about how poorly my life is going and seek to invest into someone else's.

"For where two or three have gathered together in My name, there I am in their midst." (Matthew 18:20 NASB)

I AM going to look for an opportunity this week to gather with a couple friends who love Christ, pray with them, and ask for accountability in the areas that I need to see resurrected in my life.

Chapter 4
ASSERTIVE LOVE

"We're not accustomed to occupying defensive positions.
It's destructive to morale."
– Lt. Gen. H. M. "Howlin' Mad" Smith, Iwo Jima, 1945

I f you're moving out of Phase 1, you have learned how to evaluate every rejection, offense, and misunderstanding through a lens of assertive love. Without assertive love, you will not walk in spiritual power. Without love, all spiritual "work" is null and void.

If I speak in the tongues of men or of angels, but do not have love, I am only a resounding gong or a clanging cymbal. If I have the gift of prophecy and can fathom all mysteries and all knowledge, and if I have a faith that can move mountains, but do not have love, I am nothing. If I give all I possess to the poor and give over my body to hardship that I may boast, but do not have love, I gain nothing. (1 Corinthians 13:1-2 NIV)

Let's dig a bit deeper on where spiritual power comes from practically. It does not come from going on mission trips (although mission work can be life-changing), church on Wednesday and Sunday nights, being part of the leadership team, if you use the King James instead of the Amplified, how much Greek and Hebrew you know, how great a speaker you are, or a title popped in front of your name.

Side note: If you call yourself an apostle, prophet, or prayer pope, all that means is you're willing to be the first one martyred in the room for your faith. People who walk in authentic spiritual authority don't respect you more because of a title unless you've graduated from John Hopkins as a heart surgeon or you're the President of the United States. Just saying.

The kind of spiritual power that enables you to be an overcomer and share your message with power can begin right where you are today. It comes from obedience to God in your own personal life and loving people sacrificially next. It's just that simple.

Hence, why I am talking to you about unity, dealing with rejection in your own life, and teaming right from the beginning. If you choose to let it define you, you will stay on survival mode emotionally and in your vision indefinitely. In the early church, people who were argumentative or couldn't learn how to work in a team peacefully were warned once or twice and then removed if they didn't change their attitude. A matter of fact, being divisive was actually considered a perverse sin. Now, that's pretty strong. Divisiveness was put into the category, according to Paul, of being warped and willfully sinful. (There was no, "Oh, you don't understand. He or she grew up in a difficult home.")

> But avoid foolish controversies, genealogies, arguments, and quarrels about the Law, because these things are pointless and worthless. *Reject a divisive man after a first and second admonition*, knowing that such a man is corrupt and sinful; he is self-condemned. (Italics mine) (Titus 3:9-11, BSB)

I believe rejection, offense, and independence are *spirits* with a specific assignment to keep you in a defensive mindset, which will dilute your spiritual power. I don't "see" demons (#ThankGod), but I felt like God helped me understand this mentally in this context because it forced me to confront the self-protection my emotions were reinforcing. In other words, I was agreeing with the enemy in what was going to serve me and not what would benefit others. Remember Peter?

> Peter took Him aside and began to rebuke Him. "Far be it from You, Lord!" he said. "This shall never happen to You!" Jesus turned and *said to Peter, "Get behind Me, Satan! You are a stumbling block to Me. For you do not have in mind the things of God, but the things of men."* Then Jesus told His

disciples, "If anyone would come after Me, he must deny himself and take up his cross and follow Me… (Italics mine) (Matthew 16:22-24 BSB)

If Jesus spoke directly to directional identity statements made by those closest to Him, I was going to copy that! I wasn't going to just "think a scripture" in my mind. I didn't have a Peter in my life, but the truth was I was the enemy's biggest tactic! So, I "spoke" to rejection in my life and the pain it caused me and told it to come under the blood of Christ.

Why did I go through such childlike motions? Because rejection, offense, and bitterness are not just immature choices for believers, but they keep you and me held back, guarding what we believe we have that is never really ours to control.

It truly is destructive to every bit of grace God wants to pour into your life. And here's one more thing: I don't believe you can ask God for His blessing to sit and occupy a defensive position. I mean, why would God bless sissy-sassy selfish behavior? Seriously!

You will not tap into a supernatural restraint and peace until you resist your ordinary impulse to fix, control, explain, and defend yourself. Remember, you are in an unseen battle every day. Life or death. Backwards or forwards. Past or future. Yes, it's that black and white, so every decision you make as you walk in the "spirit" must be equally as so.

You must ask the Father, Son, and Holy Spirit when you pray every day: "Who can I love unconditionally? What ground can I take back inter-generationally in my family? Who can I be sent to serve at work, in my friendships, or on the mission field? What brave action can I take today that is in alignment with the vision You have given me? Lord, help me embrace emotional vulnerability and weakness for Your kingdom!"

Just to encourage you to press on... When I was getting delivered from poverty spirits like I described above, I had some of the most unbelievable situations happen to me. Ones that seemed divinely orchestrated to put me in a position where I would have an emotional meltdown or rage at the religious hypocrisy I was encountering.

Just a few of the things that happened to me:

- I was asked by Pastor #1 who married Jay and I to leave the church for speaking in tongues and messing up his orderly service.

- Jay and I were on the first couple years of our marriage, and I was still trying to wrap my mind on how "submission" worked. (My dad offered to pay for law school because I could get paid to argue if that brings any clarification to why I was struggling.)

- I attended a spiritual "grace retreat" and blew that up so bad they had to change the by-laws after I attended to weed out pregnant women. (#bigmouth)

- Had Pastor #2 call my husband and tell him I wasn't allowed to start a prayer group that I just needed to stay home and take care of the kids. WHAT? Did he really say that?

- Started counseling and meeting with inner healing counselors to help me process why I was so angry.

It was pretty embarrassing when I look back on it. I remember thinking during this time in my life, "If God disciplines those He loves, I must be the most loved woman on the planet, because I can't go one week without some kind of confrontation." I had rejection after rejection, to the point where even the people around me said, "Becky, you are like a magnet for misunderstanding."

What I have seen as a coach is most of the time there's a combination of two things going on during this Phase. You have to learn how to develop spiritual discipline to restrain yourself from reacting (like prayer, memorization, and confession when you feel compromised) AND you have to grow practical leadership skills.

This is because typically the kind of things that leave people in a place where they can't shut their mouth, they are double-minded or super-negative, and also leave them in a place where they aren't leading themselves with peace. We will talk about that more in the next chapter.

People in this Phase don't typically communicate boundaries with grace and can have a bit of social anxiety. So, here's one of the things I noticed about myself during this season of my life. I talked about my thoughts and needs incessantly. I told people about my bad day. I told them about my dreams I had last night that I thought could be God speaking to me, I told them about how fearful I was about failing. Told them what I thought God had given me for them prophetically. People who barely knew me. I was a bit of religious nut.

I had social anxiety pure and simple and was working hard to feel needed because deep down I hadn't learned how to get my affirmation from the Lord yet. I was still struggling with rejection and hadn't learned how to just operate normally in social settings. For example, I had to learn how to ask people questions when I was in bigger meetings instead of droning on about my problems. I didn't need to share all my struggles, entertain everyone, make them happy, figure out how to solve their problem, or be the fourth part of the trinity. I bet you get exhausted just reading about how I behaved.

Here's another thing, and this was a big one for me, though it may be pretty simple to you. I expected people to read my mind. I didn't know that you couldn't expect people to respect what you aren't communicating consistently by your actions. I wanted to blame that on the devil.

I also had to learn how to pray AND work on just being clear with what I expected, instead of expecting people to just know better. Basically, I didn't realize how much passive aggressive behavior had seeped into my spiritual life until I began to actually communicate how I felt or what I wanted and watched what fear it produced for me.

Here's what it looked like for me in Phase 1: Just keeping it real so you don't feel crazy.

- Wake up 5 AM and read one passage of the New Testament with four cups of coffee. (I had four kids, two years apart, so I just drank one cup per child. Am I kidding? Maybe. Maybe not.)

- 5:30 AM. Close eyes, try and give God the 34 things that were irritating and stressing me. Bless the two people that were making me want to say the F-word though I wanted to pray the ground would open up and swallow them.

- 5:45 AM. End with scripture confession cards that irritated me because I didn't see it working fast enough.

- 8:45 PM. Ask God to forgive me for saying the F-word to husband and yelling at children. Ask Him to help me eat salad instead of a chocolate cake.

So…you're human but moving into a more divine identity. You're going to feel double-minded. It takes time to train yourself to ignore those strong negative emotions. To harness the pain of the past. So, don't *should* on yourself!

Determine though to build a reservoir of the presence of God on your life. You can do it! If you feel ADHD, that's normal. Your mind is like a mustang that's been running wild over the plains for a decade. You're going to have to harness that big boy and put a saddle on him, so you can use him properly! Don't fret if your mind wanders, just bring it back over and over again, reading one passage a day.

Pray about what's bothering you, ask for direction, confess the scriptures you have so far, and get up and don't worry about failing at being a good Christian. Jesus died and has been resurrected in your life. He started the work in you and guess what? He's going to finish it without you stressing. Just focus on Him instead of where you're falling short and return for prayer the next day. It's really not super spiritual, it's just spending enough time every day talking to God that you smell like peace instead of stress. The presence of God GROWS into your life, you don't go there!

Makes sense, right? You go into a bar and have a couple gin and tonics and you're going to leave smelling like a stank cigarette. Spend 30 minutes a day reading one passage of your Bible and praying about what's bothering you instead of worrying, and guess what? You carry the scent of calm composure. I think it has a fragrance like Fabuloso, because the maid just left your house clean, and the coffee's waiting for you WITH your milk frothed. But to the men, it probably smells like a Porterhouse steak on a hunting trip.

Besides carrying a scent of peace, you will also have a "feeling" as well as accompanying courage about how to set better boundaries in your life. God doesn't have to send an angel with blinking lights. What begins to happen is things just start coming together. You seem to just understand how to treat people and make better decisions, and you want to live with more purpose. It's natural and unforced. It's called learning how to walk in the spirit!

And hath raised us up together, and made us sit together in heavenly places in Christ Jesus: That in the ages to come he might shew the exceeding riches of his grace in his kindness toward us through Christ Jesus. For by grace are ye saved through faith; and that not of yourselves: it is the gift of God: Not of works, lest any man should boast. For we are his workmanship, created in Christ Jesus unto good works, which God hath before ordained that we should walk in them. (Ephesians 2:6-10, KJV)

You begin to simply recognize when selfishness attempts to direct your path. Most of us have experienced a situation in which a someone in our life made a fear-based decision which resulted in a mess. Or someone tried to manipulate or control us into doing what they wanted us to do, rather than what we really thought was right for us.

So, as you move out of Phase 1, your aim isn't to do everything perfect or know all the answers. It's just learning how to stop acting like you have it all together and instead be authentic. No need to be superman or superwoman because you're already accepted in the beloved!

It's the simple things that will turn you into an epic warrior like Stypulkowski who was a fighter in the Polish underground resistance movement from 1939 to 1944. This story was shared by David

Seamands in his book, *Freedom from The Performance Trap*. What a practical and yet supernatural faith!

When the war ended he was in the wrong place at the wrong time and was captured by the Russian army. He and fifteen other Poles were taken to Russia to stand trial before their war crimes court. Since some Western observers were at the trials, it was necessary to get full confessions from the men in order to convict them of their supposed treason against the state. Actually, they had helped defeat the enemy with their tactics. Now, they were being accused of helping the Nazis. Prior to the trial, the men were put under rigorous interrogation to break them mentally, emotionally, and spiritually, to destroy their integrity so they would confess to anything demanded of them. Fifteen of the sixteen men broke under the grueling pressure. Only Stypulkowski didn't. And this in spite of the fact that for 69 out of 70 nights, he was brutally questioned in a series of 141 interrogations. Not only did he endure them, but at one point his interrogator broke and had to be replaced. Over and over again, his tormentors relentlessly examined everything he had ever done, or hadn't done, and examined it for fear and guilt content. His work, marriage, family, children, sex life, church, community life, and even his concept of God. This followed weeks of starvation diet, sleepless nights, and calculated terror. Most insidious of all were the signed confessions of his BEST FRIENDS, all whom blamed him. His torturers told him his case was hopeless and as good as closed. They advised him to plead guilty, so they could lessen his sentence; otherwise, it was certain death.

But Stypulkowski refused. He said he had not been a traitor and could not confess to something that was not true. He went on to plead not guilty at his trial. Largely because of the foreign observers there, he was freed. Most impressive was the completely natural and unselfconscious way he witnessed to his Christian faith. He kept that faith alive through regular prayer, and every other loyalty was subordinated to this loyalty to Christ.

Oh, it was evident that he was not free from weakness. His accusers pointed them out to him time after time, but he was never shattered by them. The reason for his endurance was that he daily presented himself to God and to his accusers in absolute honesty. He knew he was accepted, loved of God, forgiven, and cleansed. So, whenever they accused him of some personal wrong, he freely admitted it and even welcomed it.

Again and again, he humbly said, "I never felt it necessary to justify myself with excuses. When they showed me I was a coward, I already knew it. When they shook their finger at me with filthy lewd feelings, I already knew that. When they showed me a reflection of myself with all my inadequacies, I said to them, 'But Gentlemen, I am much worse than that. For you see, I had learned it was unnecessary for me to justify myself. One had already done that for me. Christ Jesus!'"

Remember, there's a difference between just getting saved and inviting a greater lordship. It will require that you fight WHO and WHAT attempts to define you through your identity in Christ. From this point on, feeling "loved" will not come from how many compliments you get on your outfit, what you have in your bank account, whether you got that promotion at work, or how consistent you are with your goals.

It will come from drawing close to your Father through Christ in praise and prayer, confessing your shortcomings to Him, and asking Him to strengthen you for the work He has called you to! When you don't choose loving actions, it's because you have forgotten WHO you are and Who is abiding within you. It's not because you FAILED at being a good Christian!

Your Identity Work and Confession

Here are two new confessions to add to your index cards!

Father, in the name of Jesus, I thank You for strengthening me with might by Your Holy Spirit in my inner man today. I believe You are increasing my faith and ability to love others practically. Lord, I don't want to just know or quote scriptures, which is just head knowledge. I want to be illuminated to how fiercely You love me, so that I may forgive and love others as militantly. Your Word says in Titus 3 that I am to speak evil of no one, to be peaceable, gentle, and showing humility to all. I believe today You are going to open the eyes of my understanding to see Your love spiritually and to love people even who cause me great pain. That You have rescued and adopted me into Your family. I ask You to sanctify me, consecrate me, and set me aside for the work of the ministry in my present occupation. I resist all offense and navigate every assignment the enemy has to dilute my ability to love whole-heartedly. I believe You are sending me, Lord, as an ambassador for Your love. (Out of Ephesians 3:16 and Titus 3:2)

Father, thank You in the name of Jesus that I am a tree planted by the water that is sending out my roots by the stream. I will not become anxious today when stress comes because I trust You to show me gently how to stay in peace. Lord Jesus, thank You that I don't need to fear any upcoming lack or drought in my life because as long as I spend time with You daily, getting to know You, I will not fail to bear fruit and to have a grace on my life. It's not about being perfect, it's about being planted in You and among Your people. (Out of Jeremiah 17:8)

Chapter 5
CLOUDED VISION

"The bended knee is not a tradition of our Corps."
– General Alexander A. Vandergrif

What I found in Phase 2 was Satan worked overtime to remind me of who had rejected me and where I could have made better choices. His strategy? Cause me to rehearse the painful images and accompanying negative emotions over and over. It was a subtle form of torture for my spirit.

Doubt and unbelief literally made me wonder if I had mental problems and needed medication for ADHD. My mind would start reminding me of my past traumas. I would try and focus forward in faith. It was like one minute I was on top of the world with confidence, and the next day I was struggling with giving up because of lingering victimization-thinking.

The consistent raging current that ran through my heart daily was maddening. It felt like this Niagara-Falls-size potential that, if harnessed, could be non-stop Holy Ghost power. However, because I was leaking out so much faith and confidence, it instead would send me river rafting down a route I couldn't seem to tame.

I was seeing with perfect clarity as a lion slayer at 7:00 AM. By 7:00 PM, I was a little lost sheep wandering off a proverbial cliff, whimpering from the cuts and bruises from the day. If this is you right now, remember! Do everything I am telling you to do with your confessions. Do it for minimally 90 days before you even evaluate how much more clarity you have. You don't *go* into a new identity. You *grow* there!

You see, at this point, what was really happening was I confused God-given struggles that were meant to test and refine me into a larger identity, with "I AM a VICTIM" because my circumstances are painful. One day I could see who I was in Christ and where I was going clearly, the next day the whole download was fuzzy, and I was doubting I had even heard God in the first place.

Now, looking back on my own journey, and after watching my clients go through the same process, I now know this assignment is to distract and discourage them from building the discipline into their lives to solidify their leadership. Because of the victimization-thinking, they will never push themselves physically, mentally, or emotionally.

Essentially, speaking for myself, I had very little mental toughness that I applied to executing on the revelation and vision

God was giving me. The minute the day started going wrong, we had an unexpected financial crisis, I thought, "See, if God was for me and I was in God's will, I wouldn't be experiencing all this tension."

Here's the mistake most Christians make when they are new to reading their Bible and learning to follow the conviction of the Holy Spirit. It is normal Christianity for you to get tension! It helps you HAVE to build mental toughness and decrease in your flesh through self-control and discipline. Without you choosing to deny yourself and push through despite your obstacles, the Lord cannot be enlarged, and you can't take back ground that has otherwise been under the enemy's control. You have to praise when you feel depressed, get out of bed and pray when you're tired, work out when it's raining, shut your mouth when you want to bad-mouth someone, and instead bless them.

Next biggie. You're going to make mistakes and wander off the path! Don't go through life expecting perfection from yourself overnight. God's grace is big enough to help you grow in clarity and humility! Sometimes clients feel so beat up if they make a mistake and yell at their kids or oversleep their prayer time, they stop taking the actions that OVER TIME will help them BECOME someone who is faithful, consistent, and walks in wisdom. Essentially, they GIVE UP TOO QUICKLY. Build some mental toughness and perseverance! Christianity is a marathon! You're in this for the long-haul!

Little tip. Where you begin to build mental toughness is when you learn to ignore the condemnation. You're going to get bombed with it non-stop. Satan wants you to feel like you're an ax-murderer from the smallest things. Some people will even say to me, "I feel like I am going to hell because I keep failing, and God wouldn't want me on His team."

What you haven't learned yet experientially is God's love never gives up on you. His love, forgiveness, and joy over your pursuit of Him never runs out. Your ability to sin and fail is not above God's GRACE. You will face fear, maybe daily, but you won't have an identity anymore of someone who is fear-based if you keep walking in the spirit. Now, this takes work. Angels are not going to wake you up to pray at 5:00 AM, or at least they haven't for me. You have to pursue God's presence if you want it on your life, but generally I think Satan over the ages has always underestimated God's sacrificial love for us. What God has started in your life, He takes joy over polishing, so don't worry about doing the Christian life perfectly.

You see, you receive conviction while you practice God's presence in prayer daily. This is because the Word of God is a literal sword. You can't read it without it shaving, chiseling, or firing up something to conform you to Christ. This is exactly what you want! This is where you're deeply changed, and you receive compassion to be sent to the people that need to hear the very message where you have become an overcomer. I remember in the beginning, sobbing almost every time I opened up my Bible or heard a worship song. I was so performance-based and unaccustomed to God's unconditional love that it undid me to the core.

Or sometimes, you can be convicted by the Holy Spirit if you do something that will cause your conscience to be compromised. I have done this purposely, because of a crappy attitude, and accidentally. However, I learned that I didn't like the consequences of disobeying the spirit. Afterwards, I received what was most likely a very measured correction from the Lord, which gave me a greater fear of God. And boy, I had plenty of opportunities to grow in that because I was constantly messing up. I believe you will find the same thing. Like me, you will think, "Nope, not opening myself up for a hinder-part smoting. Tired of getting my butt whooped. I am tired of seeing that bush now from going around the mountain 20 times."

I remember one of the things that God dealt with me on immediately was my love for watching horror movies. I mean, come on. I was like, how bad could that be? It's fake, it's fun! I mean, shoot! My Dad was taking me to scary movies for dad/daughter time when I was a teenager. It was like great bonding time:).

So, I kept feeling every time I went to watch something scary that, "Mmmm. Maybe I shouldn't watch this." But being the hard-headed individual I was, I went ahead and did it anyway one night. It was date night, and I picked out some vampire/slasher film to watch – you know, to create more peace and grace between Jay and me:).

Jay even said to me, "Didn't God tell you to kind of not be watching this kind of stuff?"

I said, "Shut up! Don't pull the Jesus card on me," and promptly put it in the cutting edge VCR technology we had in the 80s.

About halfway through the movie I was like, "Oh, I shouldn't be watching this." It was really occultic, and I was now writhing with discomfort. I went to bed afterwards, and at midnight I had to go to the bathroom and went to get out of bed, and I couldn't walk straight. It was like I was drugged. I stumbled into the bathroom. I was trying to remember if I took a Benadryl or some kind of medication that might have made me out of it. I was saturated with this anxiety I had never felt. It was crushing.

I got into our bedroom, got back into bed, and Jay said to me, "Becky, I feel like there is something in our room." Now this was the husband who really didn't believe in the whoo-woo. It would be like John Wayne telling you that he thought there was something demonic in the room. I leapt out of bed and hit the floor repenting for not obeying the Holy Spirit. I didn't wait for Jay. It was my fault. I knew better. The Lord had clearly told me not to do this, and now I was experiencing the fruit of disobeying.

Fortunately, I had marked in my Bible some authority scriptures and began confessing the Word of God over us and our house. Jay took the movie out of the house, put it in the car, and it took us an hour to get to the point where we didn't feel a demonic presence in the room. The hair was standing straight up on the back of my head, and I have never again experienced something that while I was awake. Even Jay said he could feel something completely evil in the house. I have had other experiences that I share with my team for training purposes, but this one event rocked Jay and me so severely, we never watched another horror movie ever again. Remember, the Holy Spirit isn't out to ruin your fun. He's out to guard your peace and joy.

This is why you want to learn for yourself what God has spoken to you that keeps you right on the path He has for you and not what He tells your neighbor! The Holy Spirit knows exactly where you have been, where He needs to cover you over and where He wants to send you. You have to follow HIS leading, not a legalistic set of do's and don'ts. Just remember, when you make a mistake, what God is looking for is for you to repent and simply head back into His presence, so He can do the work instead of you trying harder. And that if it's a consistent cycle of sin for you, that you get accountability and prayer from community.

So, this stage is to make you stop implementing the actions that will help you walk in the spirit of God and gain momentum! To distract you from practicing "Your Leadership Model." It's the actions you do DAILY and without compromise that help you maintain clarity and momentum, and receive a relational grace to accomplish your vision.

Prayer and confessing the Word of God over my life daily. Exercise. Eating healthy foods and living a life of moderation. Journaling my small steps forward. Praying confessions over myself daily and memorizing the Word. This was what I had to do daily in order to not slip back into my old identity. You will have to do the same.

It was putting me in remembrance that I could trust God. These actions were purifying my carbon-monoxide-filled attitude that was poisoning my faith. It was opening the windows in a musty and dusty room. It was activating my faith. And that's the last thing the enemy wants to see happen. You setting aside time to pursue God alone in your prayer closet instead of playing video games, shopping, hobbies, lunches with friends, and self-help attempts.

Here's the challenge with this assignment. When your vision is clouded, when you compromise on what God told you, your knee is bent to the enemy. This is why understanding your identity in Christ, what it means to carry the title of a Christian, and what God has called you to purpose-wise is so important. And on a side note, here's what I have seen so many times in my coaching. People make mistakes and internalize failure as who they are identity-wise. Always focusing on where they have fallen short, instead of on focusing forward in faith by confessing the Word of God over themselves daily. I made so many mistakes, it's ridiculous. There is probably a poster in heaven with my face on it that says, "Look at God's grace! If He used Becky, He will use anyone!"

It's good to think in a results-driven way as that helps us be strategic with our actions, but if it's diluting our boldness and confidence, then we have really slipped away from stewarding what God has given us and rather are sitting in the judgement seat, which is never going to be a productive place. Even Paul said he didn't judge himself but left that to God.

> I care very little if I am judged by you or by any human court; indeed, I do not even judge myself. (1 Corinthians 4:3 NIV)

This is why in so many places in the Bible, the only thing God calls us to remember is His goodness! His works, His plans for us, and that they are good and not evil. It's because in this phase of spiritual warfare, the enemy is working overtime to make you look backwards, which only clouds your future vision, so you don't remember WHO you are and WHAT mission you are called to accomplish. And guess what? This is why so many people talk endlessly about what God has called them to and never execute. They are forward-facing, but walking backwards with their speech! Change only comes because you apply yourself daily, consistently, and with force until the transformation comes.

Here's why I shared this quote with you by General Vandergrif. Marines are mentored right from the beginning of training that they are never to bend their knee mentally or physically. They are taught to work powerfully within a team environment, but if captured by the enemy to get themselves out with no help. You see, my friend, your destiny is a fight of clarity only you can fight through. You need a team, but if it's your vision, then the group will be following your lead. You have to be willing to build the mental toughness and endurance to live a life of discipline ALONE. You never wait for a friend to go with you to obey God.

This process you're in, as uncomfortable as it is, is separating and sanctifying you to be an authentic CHRISTIAN. You cannot be an overcomer until you have developed a life of discipline. Until DISCIPLINE becomes WHO YOU ARE IDENTITY-WISE when no one is watching. That's the key. There is no day that arrives that someone puts you up on a platform and says, "Here's Becky's discipline pin." Your reward is you get to eat the fruit of what you have seen prophetically for years!

So, think about what Marine recruits go through before they graduate at Parris Island. They have to finish the Crucible. It is a 54-hour long event that begins at 3:00 AM. They march five miles to begin a series of six main events to remember (remembrance always helps build your endurance for future strength) a Medal of Honor or Navy Cross recipient. Before they begin the team challenge, they are told the story of how the individual overcame during the stress of combat despite overwhelming odds. Each recruit is required to not just follow but to lead their team members at some point. They march another 40 miles on minimal food and sleep.

Each day ends at 11 at night with the recruits cleaning their weapons, eating a small meal, and having to wake up just a few hours later. The final event is a night movement course where they are woken up at 2:00 AM, where they have to hike back to the Eagle, Globe, and Anchor Event, where they finally are called a Marine. To a Marine, it's not enough to have the courage to begin the mission, you must finish strong with confidence. This is a powerful example of why the Marines produce such strong men and women within 12 weeks of training. They are indoctrinated that they are no longer mere men and women. They are part of a brotherhood that dates back 200 years that has ALWAYS been overcomers.

Imagine if you believed that you were no longer alone. What if the tests you are currently experiencing right now with your marriage, children, work, health, and church are part of your crucible? And if you were single, that it's God's will to make you an overcomer until you found the right mate or team? What if your identity was so clear that even if you were separated from your team, you were able to stand with confidence and not bow your knee to the enemy? What if you could develop that level of focus and discipline?

What if you believed you were part of such an overcoming family that it permeated your very being and cell structure? Maybe some members of your family actually gave their life heroically in battle. Well, guess what. That's what you can have if you ask God to give it to you. That's WHO you are if you have submitted to the process of mentoring and discipleship. And this, my friend, is how you will know who is going to church and going through the motions and WHO HAS BEEN SEPARATED for the work of the ministry. They have the grace to be an OVERCOMER in spirit, soul, and body. This isn't about being separated to go to theology school. The work of the ministry can be done as a janitor or while you're working at a gas station. This is about learning how to obey God fully, right where you're at today.

This line of thinking doesn't come from being a perfect Christian. It comes from lordship. And when you make mistakes, repenting quickly, and then returning quickly to the presence of God. You do this over and over, daily, until you walk in more liberty and more peace. But here's what I want you to know. You're going to have to FIGHT for this through your authority if you come out of a family generationally that has been saturated with idolatry, occult activities, and narcissism. You can't compare yourself to someone who grew up in a home with stable parents under Lordship. It's like giving a mustang to a professional horse trainer to develop or a carpooling mom of five. Which one do you think is going to develop the calm, focused trail horse? Give yourself grace, but understand it's completely possible to breakthrough if you're willing to block the time and do the work.

This means in all the places your parents or grandparents didn't know how to or didn't want to develop the discipline to take ground in, this is now your giant to slay. This isn't a curse, it's a blessing. You're receiving a personal invitation from Christ Himself to make your name great through HIM.

You know what creates a great name according to the scripture? It's not your ability to build wealth. It's not how many people like your status on Facebook or Instagram. It's not how clean your house is or how many job promotions you get this year. It's not being a perfect parent (thank You, Jesus). It's what you activate your FAITH to believe for. It's the place that your heart faints in. It's your dream desire that Satan tells you is all about you.

For Abraham, that was having children that were his own. Think about that. He could've adopted a million, but he desired his own children, and God called that righteous because it required faith. His wife laughed at the idea.

For David, that was defending his family's and friends' honor. Satan, through his family, called him arrogant and prideful, but he knew what God had already done through him. Your past wins position you for future giants, which is why you have to build this into your life!

For Deborah, that was being bold enough to articulate instructions to a MILITARY GENERAL about timing, strategy, and his fear of failure.

God doesn't always use the predictable or people we are comfortable with to bring out the victory. If you're a white man, He may send a black woman to you. If you're a doctor with a Ph.D., He may send a mechanic who works on your car. Spiritual authority is not a race, intelligence, or position. Never tell God who He can send into your life, and don't miss your divine breakthrough because you judged the messenger He sent.

For Peter, that was sharing WHO Christ was to the religious establishment, what he had done through receiving HIM as Lord, and not worrying about what kind of persecution he received because of it.

You see, my friend, FAITH is the Word of God in due season in your practical challenge. It's what you are believing for and to see happen that will give God glory. Whether it's children, bringing down the Goliath of addiction in your family, stepping into the authority level God has really called you to, or sharing with your co-workers the work of Christ in your life… It all requires FAITH and for you to begin to COMMAND your kingdom and queendom with authority.

You will begin increasing in your rulership by confessing WHO you are and where you are going. As you do this consistently, you will BECOME identity-wise a force to be reckoned with. You will find that when you experience rejection or fear, instead of running to the fridge to eat, smoke, or get on the phone and complain about the person, you will instead BLURT out your identity and watch your IDENTITY and LEADERSHIP IN CHRIST become solidified. Expect the tension, warfare, and rejection. It's part of the tests that are going to turn you into a lean, mean, fighting machine for Jesus.

Your Identity Work and Confession

Lord Jesus, by faith I understand that the universe was formed at God's command, so that what is seen was not made out of what was visible. I want to walk in Your identity in my leadership, which is commanding LIFE to begin out of voids of darkness and chaos.

Walking by what I see internally about who I am in YOU and where You have called me to and not by what my family, my friends, or my finances dictate to me. I will increase in the fear of the Lord and decrease in the fear of man's opinions today. Lord, give me one obstacle this week to apply my faith to overcome. I AM becoming a consistent, faithful leader by Your grace. I AM being sanctified and set aside for the work of the ministry in my vocation today. Give me an opportunity today to share Your work in my life. I WILL smile at everyone today. I WILL guard my peace and choose to rule my kingdom/queendom with discipline, integrity, and grace. You discipline those You love, and this makes a son or daughter, not performing perfectly. I will say "no" to anything that distracts me from my leadership model I am building which is prayer, exercise, and applying myself to build the vision in this season You have called me to put my hands to. Lord, I will do the work, obey, and sacrifice accordingly as You suffered, learned obedience, and allowed the Father to perfect You through Your temptations and trials.

I will not bow my knee to the enemy today. I have been given authority to trample on serpents and scorpions and over all the power of the enemy. (Luke 10:19)

I AM an overcomer by the blood of the Lamb and the word of my testimony. I love my life not even unto death. (Revelation 12:11)

No weapon formed against me shall prosper, and every tongue that rises up against me in judgement I shall refute for this is the heritage of those who love the Lord. (Isaiah 54:17)

I resist chaos and voids in my life, and I ask You, Holy Spirit, to brood over my vision with me. I AM coming out of darkness and confusion into your marvelous light and liberty! (1 Peter 2:9)

Chapter 6
LEARNING TO PROCESS PAIN

"You cannot allow any of your people to avoid the brutal facts. If they start living in a dream world, it's going to be bad."
– Retired Marine General James Mattis, United States Secretary of Defense

This quote was directed at leadership within Marine Command when Mattis was a general. I thought it highly appropriate for our focus because in Phase 2, you might begin (or have already been) receiving spiritual warfare that attempts to create escapist responses to emotional pain.

This is a huge sabotage to you leading boldly. When we are in emotional pain we have a temptation to harden our hearts by taking vindictive actions or medicating ourselves. I mean, who likes to feel like they are bleeding all over the place emotionally? No one. But the truth is it's better to appear vulnerable and rely on the Holy Spirit than harden your heart with independence.

The enemy's objective in this stage is to keep you fantasizing about the control you could have. You know. We have all done it. Someone says something offensive to you. On your way home from work, you rehearse it in your mind, and instead of walking away quietly this time, you come up with some pithy comment that stops them in their tracks. Or, maybe you're fearful about terrorist coming into your workplace because you have been traumatized by violence before. Maybe you're always seeing in your mind's eye yourself emerging in a flash with your gun drawn or other demonstrative showy responses that overtake the bad guys.

Essentially, this is when we engage in vain imaginations. It's big on the enemy's tactic list. He entices us to process our emotional pain through escapism. When we learn how to recognize this and instead choose to pray in the spirit or take healthy practical action, we experience His supernatural provision in the midst of oppression.

This is the part of coaching where people have hit a wall, and when I start digging down, they describe to me a trauma that has caused them pain. This in turn leads to a lack of clarity with their vision or that they "know what to do but they aren't doing it." Here are some of the signs I ask my clients to look for.

- Continually oversleeping so that they miss the opportunity to engage in the activities that lead them into their vision.

- Activities that are fun and give them an opportunity to socialize but distract them from the vision they want to implement.

- Overeating to medicate emotional pain or not eating in a way they are convicted about. They might be between 10 or 200 pounds overweight.

- Playing video games or computer games in the car, at work, at night.

- Alcohol that is not maintained in moderation. Our liberty should not become a license to sin.

- A work or home environment that is so cluttered with junk or animals it's not healthy for you or it creates distraction.

- Addictions (drugs, pornography, shopping, gambling, serious self-harm behaviors)

A big indicator that this is actual spiritual warfare is there is no practical reason for you to want or need to continue in these patterns or it's plain harmful to you. You're just engaging in them because you feel hopeless, depressed, or you have tried and can't seem to change by yourself. Usually along with these choices, clients have no accountability in prayer or anyone asking them hard questions. This is because Satan always encourages people to hide once he ensnares them with shame. Feeling compromised is always an indicator that you need to walk out into the light, pray the prayer of confession with your accountability partner, and begin your healing.

Here's another sabotage, though not as noticeable that I see in this phase. People will get fantastic ideas, share them with others, but not execute them. (And I mean BRILLIANT business or ministry strategies). They do this so many times, people begin to point this out to them and they begin to see themselves as someone who has great ideas that nothing ever comes out of. So, they live in the land of potential not purpose. This becomes HUGELY frustrating to them. They become a "dreamer" in their own eyes and other people's eyes. They enter into a never-ending season of "it's just around the corner." The reason they are dealing with a lack of execution is because they haven't invited real biblical mentoring into their life that is challenging them. They can't ask other people to execute on their vision because they are hiding themselves! In other words, you can't ask others to step up to the plate if you haven't been doing that yourself in humility. It's an identity issue at the core!

Invariably, if I am coaching someone in Phase 2, and I ask them about their leadership model and if they are very disciplined with it, they will say no they don't have this in place. Or they used to do it but not anymore. This sometimes happens when people experience church splits or divorce and they have to start building a new identity by themselves again. I want to share something very important with you. The devil doesn't care if you dream big and talk about what you're going to do or where you're going. What threatens him is a disciplined life that is accountable to small actions and authentically transparent. Never be afraid of starting over. Remember Job. Sometimes you can do all the right things and still have everything burnt to the ground. But remember, a short time after Job's difficulty, he experienced RESURRECTION and MULTIPLICATION in every area. God loves making your latter days greater than your former days. I love how the Apostle James breaks it down for us so practically.

> But he who looks into the perfect law of liberty and continues in it, and is not a forgetful hearer but a doer of the work, this one will be blessed in what he does. If anyone among you thinks he is religious, and does not bridle his tongue but deceives his own heart, this one's religion is useless. Pure and undefiled religion before God and the Father is this: to visit orphans and widows in their trouble, and to keep oneself unspotted from the world. (James 1:25-27, NKJV)

Whenever I get overwhelmed, I always return to the basics. I ask myself, "Have I been doing my confessions and blocking time for prayer? Have I been exercising daily? Am I executing on the vision God has given me? Am I serving well in my marriage and family?"

Within everyone's yearly vision plan should be a focus for connecting with people in your family who feel "less than." All families have the individuals that are considered black sheep or have made poor decisions. In some families, there are widows or abandoned children that have fallen through the cracks due to divorce. We are told biblically that if we don't take care of widows we are worse than heathens! I really encourage making oppressed individuals in your family a ministry focus, as it helps people who are unsaved in your family see that you have a practical faith. You're Jesus with skin on. What good does it do you to support people across the world and then not take care of the lonely in your own family? Let's have an authentic faith. We can do both.

Before we end this chapter, I want to talk to you about the power of worship to process pain. If people really understood what happens spiritually when they worship God, they would do it much more often when they are in pain or feeling desperate. They would use this as a number one go-to instead of reading self-help books and the other stuff we do to try to figure out how to fix our lives.

First of all, it's a military strategy, and it completely routes the enemy. In ancient Israel, the worshippers actually were sent out BEFORE THE ARMIES. The walls of Jericho were pulled down through praise. As a personal testimony, I experienced the presence of God in my room twice in my life during times I set aside for worship. Being in the presence of God ruins you for the ordinary.

One of the times, I was in tormenting emotional pain and couldn't seem to break through it. Part of the challenge was I was so angry with the people involved with the situation and I couldn't see any resolution. I was praying and asking God for wisdom and patience.

Friends couldn't help me process through it. Counseling wasn't solving it. I was at wit's end. In the problem I was dealing with, I was freaking out because I felt so out of control and trapped. I could see no change was going to happen, and the alternatives in either direction weren't good. I needed peace. I set aside a couple hours when my kids were at Mother's Morning Out, and I put on worship music and just sang along with the songs, like I was singing just for Jesus alone in His court.

Now, I know this is going to sound corny, but I put on one of the nicest night gowns I had (and by that I mean it wasn't flannel, because I was homeschooling at the time...no flannel for Jesus LOL), and I started dancing. I sang badly. Danced probably worse than that, and after about an hour, I could feel something begin to change in the room.

The presence of God is hard to describe, but even after 25 years I can remember it like it was yesterday. I completely stopped moving around because it enveloped me. No mist. No sparkles. No angels. Couldn't see anything practically that had changed, but I felt this presence. This all happened physically in the room, and simultaneously in my mind suddenly along with the change in my perception level. It was supernatural.

I "heard"... "I AM here. Ask Me any question you want, and I will answer you."

In a split second, I responded with, "Why did you do nothing when I was in pain as a child?"

And then the Holy Spirit said, as I felt His presence barely touch my cheekbone... "I was never this far away from you. You were never alone."

I sobbed and sobbed.

And here's the thing. I had no idea that the conflict internally I felt, the loss of control, was related to this childhood pain. Never realized that deep down spiritually and emotionally I felt like I was on my own. That I had to figure everything out for myself. Didn't realize that I just didn't know how to trust God or didn't want to because my earthly father was so unpredictable.

And He didn't say anything else after that, and I didn't either. I just sat there in silence that the God of the universe would visit me and answer a question I had. God's like that. You think you need one thing, and He comes in and says, "Oh by the way…you were totally bound up in FEAR, and what you thought was the problem wasn't the problem."

In this particular situation, I was trying to obey God, but I was so engrained with taking control that the wrestling match was causing a serious emotional problem for me. I hadn't learned yet to pray and pace myself. To communicate boundaries and then give people time to change.

A couple days later I thought to myself, *I had God in the room. I should have asked him a little deeper theological question than something all about my childhood.*

I had another time where the Holy Spirit came in during worship like that, and I just stopped. To be honest, I have found God isn't much of a talker. The times I have really experienced the presence of the Lord, it was a tangible weight on me. I could ask Him a question or two, and then He would just stop talking, and I was illuminated by His love on how to proceed.

I didn't share this with you to make you think I was more spiritual than you. I wanted to share this experience with you because this is what God wants with you. He wants you to come to Him and worship when you're in emotional pain, so He can answer any question you have on your heart. I have found that God doesn't wait for us to get more together emotionally, get more spiritual, go to church, get more disciplined or get more delivered before He visits us. He just waits for us to get desperate enough to turn off the TV, get babysitting for the kids, and instead of going shopping, pursue Him. We can all be as close to God as we want to be.

Your Identity Work and Confession

Father, thank You that no temptation has come into my life but that which is NORMAL for everyone. (1 Corinthians 10:13) You are faithful. You make a way out of every temptation I receive so that I can stay self-disciplined and have my conscience clear before you. Lord, open my eyes during temptation so that I can see what specific actions to take to stay conformed to my identity in Christ. Thank You that I AM walking in the leadership You have preordained for me before the foundation of the world. I AM someone who lives above reproach – not self-absorbed, not quick tempered, not given to drunkenness, not violent, not greedy for money. I AM a people person, I AM someone who hosts get-togethers and events at my home that increase everyone's joy. I love good works, I AM DISCIPLINED, and I AM SELF-CONTROLLED and CONSISTENT. Thank You, Lord Jesus, when I catch myself thinking of stressful or fearful things, I will think on something that brings me joy or is kind. (Philippians 4:8) I will discipline my mind. Holy Spirit, I invite You to correct me and bring to my attention anything that does not line up with what will help me be a peace-giver in other people's lives. I declare over myself that I will worship God in spirit and in truth. (John 4:21) I will discipline my mind to know the Word of God and yet engage You with my emotions. I bow my knee and my will to the Lord Jesus Christ in spirit and truth.

Add this card to your confession arsenal.

Chapter 7
PRACTICAL POWER

"Since I first joined the Marines, I have advocated aggressiveness in the field and constant offensive action. Hit quickly, hit hard, and keep right on hitting. Give the enemy no rest, no opportunity to consolidate his forces and hit back at you."
– Lt. Gen. H. M. "Howlin' Mad" Smith

In Phase 2, you might still be dealing with passivity and poverty mindsets such as not being able to create a compelling vision, passive-aggressiveness, and enabling the idolatry other people are engaged in. Biblical success happens when we come to the place where we help others build significant lives, not by fame or fortune.

When people are unable to live bold lives, it usually boils down to an identity issue that they feel conflicted with. I believe with all my heart that every person has a purpose that, when they dig down and do the work to identify it, will propel them into an impactful kingdom life. We can only achieve this through receiving Christ, receiving His love, and then using our gifts and talents to serve others. Everyone has gifts from God, and this is the phase where you should be doing the work to identify them and grow them rather than hiding your talents.

One of the first things I look for if people cannot seem to be consistent with their vision is how solidified their boundaries are, if they can confront correctly, and if they are living within their core values. These can cause your identity to be diluted and you to feel conflicted. One minute, you're in with a kingdom vision and the next you're disturbing your own peace because you're not handling tension correctly.

Many times, people confuse giving others grace with not enforcing their own personal boundaries. The bottom line is if you don't respect yourself enough to safeguard your time and vision and consequently teach people how to treat you, you're going to get a lot more drama than other people. You walk in peace, righteousness, and joy by making a choice to build a godly life. People who don't want to live a compelling life are very resentful of others who do. Jealousy can drive people to intimidate you into responding to their needs and not what God has illuminated to you is His will for your life. They can choose chaos, not having good friends who love them, and crisis living, which is what goes along with not being in the will of God. Here's the thing. The enemy knows when you're fearful, not clear, or not committed to enforcing your boundaries, so he will do whatever he can to bring these individuals into your life. It's idolatry to fear man's opinion of you rather than what God says about you identity-wise.

Remember, God makes a way EVERY TIME when you're under temptation to do what you have to do to stay in peace and within your vision. However, you have to radically confront people who don't have good boundaries, and if you can't, then get the training you need to stop enabling their idolatry.

There is something about dealing with people that choose chaos that makes us feel vulnerable. It was extremely hard for me to process through the fear of man and learn how to communicate with clarity what I felt was right and what I expected from people when I was in this phase. I threw up. I had headaches. I overate and drank to medicate my fear. But God was faithful to deliver me, and He will deliver you, too, if you don't give up.

To be honest, looking back, I don't believe I really started walking in my boldest identity zones until I learned how to write, pray, and articulate my vision and avoid passive-aggressive behaviors. This required me to say "no" to well-meaning agendas. I lost friendships that I expected were going to last a lifetime. It was painful.

After that, I was always being asked to join a team, serve, or do other things that sapped my time. It was like I was attacked with guilt for not investing time in other people's vision or needs. One day, when I felt especially conflicted, the Lord said to me, "Becky, do you think that person's vision is more valuable to Me than what I have called you to? Because when you stand before Me, I won't be asking you about theirs. I will be asking you what you did with your talents, giftings, and time. Did you hide yours because you thought I was a hard task master, or did you know My heart for you and leap towards obeying Me in what you were gifted at?"

So, I can tell you, you take ground offensively from the enemy when you feel the most vulnerable, not when you feel strong and courageous. It's really hard to come to the place where you say "no" without guilt. And it takes time to walk in a confidence of WHO you are and WHERE you're going. But when you begin to see the fruit of radically obeying God with your own vision, you will know it was worth all the tension you received to stand in your boldest identity zone.

The work to discover these two things will enable you to love assertively through rejection and take constant offensive action towards walking in authentic kingdom power. Also, when we are actively engaged in fulfilling our purpose and we stay within our core values, we are less likely to give the enemy an opportunity to gain a foothold in our lives. You don't have to work at being in the will of God. You flow through the good to the acceptable and then into the perfect will of God for your life.

Here's a key to remember so that you can walk in the authority that God has called you to and quit enabling other people's poor choices. Our aim is to be like Jesus. Remember He gave grace but ALWAYS REQUIRED His closest partners to be willing to live sacrificially. Faith and works. Compassion and calling. You can't have one without the other.

Jesus was always initiating conversations that challenged people to take action and to follow Him immediately. That minute. Not when the time was better. Not when they had more resources. Not when it wasn't so public or obvious. Not if they got offended or they didn't. He was and still is the king of what I call the "fish or cut bait" moment, as in ACTION. And He really wasn't worried too much about saying it in a politically correct or feel-good way. People who walk with God closely will always be asking you to do bigger things and to ditch mediocrity.

Let's review.

- Woman caught in the ACT of adultery. GRACE to you, but sin no more. (As in change this second.)

- Jesus walking by the Sea of Galilee saw two brothers. Follow Me now, and I will make you fishers of men.

- Woman at the well. Go and get your husband. (Didn't pray she would engage Him if it was God's will. He engaged her purposely.)

- To Zacchaeus. I want to have a party at your house today. Go, get it ready!

- To the disciple who wanted to bury his father. Follow Me now, and let the dead bury their dead.

- The Pharisees and scribes ask for a sign. Not doing anything for you. An evil generation wants signs. You can have the sign of Jonah.

- To Peter when he didn't want Jesus to die. Get behind me. You're an offense, Satan. (Imagine us saying that to people that want to encourage us to not fulfill the vision He gave us.)

- Man with unclean spirit. Be quiet, and come out of him.

- Levi the tax collector. Follow Me right now.

- To the scribes. Not forgiving trash-talking against the Holy Spirit. You, my religious friend, I will send to hell.

- Woman with issue of blood. Who touched me? Great. You're well; go in peace.

- To the disciples. I want to feed this crowd. How are we going to do it? You do it now.

- To Peter. Who do you say I am? "You're the Christ." (Good answer.)

- To the tree that wasn't bearing fruit. Let no one eat fruit from you ever again. One-day result. Because when Jesus showed up and needed it, it had nothing to give. WHOA! Let that be a lesson for us on doing whatever it takes to be prepared.

- To disciples. If you don't forgive, I won't forgive you. Want to be the leader? Be the best servant now.

- To the paralytic. Your sins are forgiven. Get up and walk.

- To the widow. Quit crying. Get up, kid!

- To the disciples when they were afraid. Have some faith. And He rebuked the wind.

- To the thief on the cross. You're forgiven now. You will be with Me today in Paradise.

I believe we are in great danger of missing God's will for our lives by praying on things too long. When God sends someone to challenge you, you better be ready to jump. I see more people who are fear-based and use prayer as an excuse to procrastinate. Did I say that out loud? Whoops… Or they get offended when I require them to make a quick decision. The truth is you don't need a lot of time to make a right choice. It's almost always fear of lack and what people will think about us that holds us back from bold actions.

Do you want to walk in a demonstration of God's anointing in your life? Then you have to do the work to align yourself to receive the *dunamis* power of God. Remember when Mary said to the angel, "How can it be that I will become pregnant with Christ?" The angel said to her, the DUNAMIS is going to come upon you. Mary had to AGREE with what was spoken to her in a "suddenly" moment.

Imagine if she would have said, "Hmmmm. I need to pray about this. Can you come back next week?" She seized the moment and said, "BE IT UNTO ME AS YOU HAVE SAID," not worrying about what anyone was going to think or say about her. You see, my friend, you can't have power, might, and strength on your life until you stop worrying about what people think about your actions. You can't receive *dunamis* without assertive and bold instant action.

Dunamis is a Greek word, and it is your choice to create it in your life. It isn't available to just super spiritual people. It's for everyone who wants to take bold action and implement boundaries strategically by following the Holy Spirit. It is used 121 times in the Bible, and it always centers around assertive action and wonderful transformational change.

One of the things that will really dilute the dunamis in your leadership is passive-aggressive behaviors. It will kill your clarity and momentum, and the truth is YOU are responsible as a Christian to guard your peace. If you don't do that, you won't grow a bold identity as a Christian!

At the heart of this behavior in your life is a lack of leadership or ability to ask the questions that will bring clarity to fear. Typically, people who are passive-aggressive have grown up in homes where one parent was controlling or addictive, and the other parent was passive or an enabler. This person is usually SATURATED with idolatry, and it won't come down without you really being willing to stand through the tension.

Passive-aggressive people expect to be disrespected or taken advantage of eventually, so they jump to conclusions when there is the least amount of miscommunication or mistakes made. They BELIEVE they are disrespected at the core of their identity, and it's become WHO THEY ARE IDENTITY-WISE. They are also great at excuse-making about their behavior, which is why it takes so much energy and time to deal with these kinds of people. If this is in your response patterns, you have to get militant about addressing this, as it has most of the time been in your family for generations. Most of the time if it's addressed, they not only deny it but turn it around so that you feel shamed or doubt you saw it.

Passive-aggressive leaders surround themselves with enablers, so it's classic crazy town banana pants feeling for anyone who attempts to address it. The challenge in business is that time is money. So honestly, you have to evaluate if this is the kind of partnership you want in your life, as it's a massive financial leak to your profits and marketing.

How do you know you're dealing with a leader or business owner who is passive-aggressive? Here are some characteristics:

- They tell you they are going to take care of it but "forget" regularly.

- They triangulate to others in the family or team rather than directing their questions to the person who can change the situation.

- Everything seems fine, and then all of a sudden, they just email you about how disappointed they are with you or your performance.

- They keep pushing the boundaries until you explode because they don't want to be the one who initiated the conflict.

- They ask you to deal with confrontation for them because they are too busy, or you are "great" at being diplomatic.

- They won't deal with individuals one on one but rather address the offense in a group setting by alluding to the problem.

- You will hear them always complain about how they are not respected, or they just keep getting taking advantage of over and over again.

- They cut people off relationally, but then when they see them publicly in front of others they pretend all is well.

- They show favorites depending on who is affirming them.

- They can point out every little detail of how you failed but don't take any ownership in how they failed to lead.

- They always have an excuse for why they couldn't finish a project or why it didn't work out.

So how do you deal with these kinds of friends, business acquaintances, and family members in your life? First of all, address their behavior as passive-aggressive, but guard your heart and time with them! If you decide to confront them, have in mind the decision or action you will be taking ahead so that you get to put it in play.

Next, don't second-guess yourself. Passive-aggressive people have a way of making you feel like it's your fault when they are minimizing or manipulating you. Pray for them to receive the truth but again, don't come under the fear they try to intimidate you with. Limit your time with them unless they acknowledge their issues.

Lastly, and this is the most important. You HAVE to set very clear boundaries with them without guilt. If they are attempting to control you, just let them know up front precisely what actions you will be taking and then EXECUTE every time. If you don't, you have taught them that you are negotiable.

What I want you to understand is this kind of power can be yours, BUT it will require you to endure hardship, get set free from people-pleasing, and pursue your vision daily.

Jesus has already given you a mandate to walk in dunamis. YOU have to agree with it and then take bold action.

"He now called the Twelve together and gave them power ("dunamis") and authority to overcome all the devils and to cure diseases, and sent them to proclaim the kingdom of God and to heal."

Now, let's add some dunamis confessions to your arsenal.

Your Identity Work and Confession

Father, thank You that You have given me power to bring everything under the blood that creates fear for me. I will not ponder on the past. I will write down and talk about where I am going vision-wise. Right now, in the name of Jesus, I declare the insight and illumination to bring great boundaries and peace into my day. I will not fret or worry. Instead I will pray and ask You to give me the tools and strategies to navigate any chaos the enemy brings to me. I declare no weapon formed against me will prosper, and every tongue that rises up against me will fail. I will not ask everyone what they think I should do. I will pray, listen to what I think You are saying to me, and ask one or two people I trust if that confirms to them. I AM becoming a force to be reckoned with in the kingdom of God. (Luke 10:19)

Holy Spirit, I invite You into my day to rule and reign over my small choices and the bigger ones. I ask You to anoint me with dunamis power so that I can testify for You with great effect to the people in my family, to the people I work with, and throughout my nation. (Acts 1:8)

Lord Jesus, You are the author and finisher of my faith. I ask You to give me a joy to endure the hardship necessary to see the vision You gave me to come to pass, so that when I see You, I can hear, "Well done, good and faithful steward. Enter into the rest I have for you." (Matthew 25:23)

Chapter 8
THE TRUTH-BEARER TEST

"A good plan, violently executed now, is better than a perfect plan next week."
– Gen. George Patton, Jr., U.S. Army General

You are now entering into the third phase of spiritual warfare. Here the Holy Spirit is aligning you to be a bold truth-bearer with your specific testimony. This is why it makes no difference how many people have published books on prayer, addiction and deliverance, or marriage. When you tell your story, this produces an anointing because this is how Christ was magnified in your life. Your story is powerful for the kingdom because it was how you overcame!

This happened because you have taken time to memorize the Word of God, yielded to the lordship of Christ, and haven't been able to be uprooted in your focus due to offense. Now the spiritual warfare comes because you are being elevated to tell your testimony to more people.

You have taken another step into your destiny and are growing in confidence as you trust your Father to establish and send you with your unique message focus. You will always receive spiritual tension for sharing how you overcame through Christ rather than a worldly strategy or brand. For example, let's say you're 30 pounds overweight. Praying and asking God for a healthy eating and exercising pattern vs. a brand or product you use will give you spiritual warfare when you lose the weight, and people ask you how you did it. Anything that gives the Lord the glory and gives an opportunity for you to share specific scriptures and lordship principles is going to align you for spiritual resistance. Don't back up, just expect it!

Now again, I don't want to purposely offend you, but the Lord will not share His glory with brands or organizations. The more you understand that programs, positions, titles, and degrees come through positional authority delegated to you, the easier it will be to not rely on that for spiritual authority or leadership. You also won't be uprooted during shakeups when they come.

This is at the root when you hear people talk about Jesus who are in delegated positional authority, but they seem to carry no tangible power, aren't making disciples, and can't seem to ever receive breakthrough. It's because they are relying on man-made traditions and positions rather than building influence God's way, which is through applying their identity in Christ to overcome through trials, suffering, and persecution.

The kind of authority that makes you a truth-bearer comes from receiving your Father's affirmation, obeying His instructions alone, and standing strong through the spiritual warfare the enemy brings you. Especially the warfare you get through the body of Christ, as unfortunately the enemy will use this as well.

This is one of the phases where you will receive intense pressure, because here you are becoming an actual THREAT to Satan. You have learned how to live a sacrificial life, pray, worship through pain, forgive freely despite the injustice, and now have become a force for the kingdom of God. Generals in the courts of God are not made through their thesis writing ability, their oratory skills, or a degree. They are made through suffering and coming out boldly carrying the message of how they overcame through Christ. And what you need to know right now is that if you want to fulfill the mandate to make disciples, it's your job to create tension for the enemy by being a truth-bearer in your family, friendships, job, and church.

Truth-bearers apply their identity, boundaries, and spiritual giftings in everyday problems so that the Holy Spirit can convict people's hearts to the point where they have to yield to the work Christ is trying to do in the situation at hand, or they must deny Him entrance. There is no in-between, and to try to stand in both camps will do nothing but steal your peace and dilute your spiritual authority.

The Word of God says in Romans that the law is written in our hearts, and our conscience bears witness. Everyone's message is very unique, handcrafted for them by the Holy Spirit. So, what the Lord gives you liberty for, He may not give me liberty for. And vice-versa. What boundaries the Lord gives me to strictly adhere to may not be a conviction issue for you. We all need to work out our salvation with fear and trembling, taking into consideration the message that we know God is cultivating in our lives.

This tweaking of a life message and training situations that bring about the weight of authority on your marketplace mentoring or ministry are not built overnight. In some cases, it takes decades. This is because it takes time for the people around you to see how you respond to pressure, the strategies you feel led to take to overcome chaotic situations, and the results you receive. In other words, what you say God told you does not matter as much as the results that come about because of how you obeyed the Lord. If you heard God, the fruit will begin to manifest for all to see, and your calling will increase as you steward the gifts of the spirit in your life. Remember, more authority comes with greater maturity.

If you have had a lack of spiritual mothering or fathering in your life that has left you wounded, this phase could be prolonged because you are having to learn how to hear God accurately and push through the fear of man. There is something very innate within all of us that desperately cries out to be pleasing to our God and know we are special to Him. If we have not trained ourselves and become accustomed to a daily discipline of listening to the affirmation of our Father, we can inadvertently become a man-pleaser because we are so desperate to feel affirmed by father and mother figures in our lives. This can cause significant problems for you in the workplace and also in the ministry.

One of the most significant lessons I learned from the Lord was within the first decade of my walk with Christ. I had developed a daily discipline of prayer and journaling, but then when I was faced with a real-life obstacle, I would pray, hear God but then not take action because I felt the need to ask permission before I executed. In this phase, God dealt with me over and over again about moving forward even if I got resistance from other people or my plan was too simple.

I had to go through a long, convoluted process of learning how to hear God, obey HIM, and leave the results to HIM. I have a personal story I want to share with you that was part of this phase.

In the beginning of my marriage, specifically the first ten years, I had a deep-seated need for men to approve me from the lack of fathering I received. I constantly struggled with overt rebellion to authority figures, and then alternatively engaging in public drama to garner attention. No in-between for me. Oh, it was sad to watch. Thankfully, my husband and one or two mentors were very patient with me spiritually and emotionally, as it was pretty taxing to my husband as he had to constantly deal with people telling him to get his wife into line!

Growing up in an addiction-based home left me having to be responsible for myself emotionally at a young age, but my heart even as an adult craved guidance from male father figures. When I got married in my early twenties, it was really difficult to trust my husband for guidance and yet obey the Lord in situations where frankly I knew I had heard God clearly. On top of this, I had picked up along the way (somewhere) that if I was truly spiritual and trusted God, I would go along with whatever the person in authority over me told me to do.

God was trying to get me personally to a place where I learned how to trust what I heard from Him and communicate it effectively so that I experienced eating the fruit of my labor in prayer. Also, if no one has mentored you personally or shared this with you, please let me support you with this truth.

God cares about YOU (men and women) understanding how to carry authority and at the level He has called you to, and conflict is part of the emotional price you will have to work through to share the message God wants you to share and that will bring healing to people and situations God's way. Additionally, it's normal to receive tension when God is rearranging organizational structures and people aren't willing to follow where the Holy Spirit wants to take them individually and corporately.

One of the first places I began to feel resistance in this phase was with Jay, my husband, as we were both needing to learn what it meant to recognize each other's spiritual giftings. Mine are more confrontational because I have a gifting to help people pioneer out of chaos and create models, while Jay carries more of a governmental grace where he can resolve conflict, is extremely stable, and is a friend to everyone! Now, before I tell you this story, I want to tell you in Jay's defense that up to this point he had done a lot of mop up relational work for me. In other words, I was frequently shooting my mouth off and not responding in love, so the hubs was getting a little worn out with my "calling."

It was about this time that the Lord wanted to do some work in my life to help me see the fruit to my prayers. We had four young children at the time and drove them around in a Toyota Previa that apparently was never supposed to have problems with air conditioning because the windows only cracked out an inch for ventilation. The air conditioning on this van went out two times on us, and the third time, it was the middle of July in Tallahassee, Florida. Not Alaska. It was not just hot, it was a literal oven. I would leave for the grocery store at 8 AM, and in 30 minutes the kids would look like they had heat stroke.

So, no money for air. Four kids under eight. Not using credit cards. I was homeschooling. I had three kids in the back with one-inch window openings, and Joe in a baby seat. During the Tallahassee summer. Not Alaska. It was not just hot. It was suffocating, so I began to pray about how we were going to solve this problem.

Day 1:

Me: "The kids look like turnips in the back seat, Lord. I need some money to get the air fixed."

Jesus: "Take the van into the dealership and get a quote so you can get it fixed."

Me: "We have no money for the quote they were going to give us, that is not a good plan."

I shared with Jay what I felt like the Lord had told me and he said, "Becky, there is no point in doing that because we don't have the money for the repair right now. We need to wait and save the money."

Day 2:

Me: "Lord, we have an air conditioning problem."

Jesus: "Yes, I can see that."

Me: "What should I do?"

Jesus: "I gave you a plan and told you what to do."

Me: "The husband You gave me did not like that plan."

Jesus: "Oh, I am sorry. I thought you were asking Me for a plan, not Jay."

Me: "Ommppfff. Oh dear. Houston, we have a problem."

Me: "Now, Lord. You tell me to obey my husband. My husband told me to wait."

Jesus: "Okay. Stay hot."

Me: "This is not theological correct. You realize that, right?"

Jesus: (Looks at me and doesn't answer.)

I went to run errands and ran into an older business man who attended our church, and he asked me how we were doing.

I said, "Fine, except for my turnip kids." He laughed, and I told him about our air challenge. I told him what I thought God had told me, and how I was struggling with whether to move forward because Jay didn't feel great about it.

He told me, "Hang in there! I will be praying for you to have wisdom and for provision!"

I drove around for another week, and then I started to get really mad. I knew I had prayed. I knew what God told me, and I knew what the husband told me. I couldn't stand to see my kids hot like that. So I woke up, prayed, put all the four kids in the car, and walked into the dealership.

Salesman: "Can I help you?"

Me: (Four sweaty kids behind my denim homeschooling 1980s dress. I start crying.) "I HAVE NO AIR. My husband is going to be so mad at me when he knows I am here. I don't have money to get this fixed, but I prayed and felt like God told me to bring it here."

Salesman: (Pity look for crazy woman who has too many kids and is probably having nervous breakdown from stress.) "Oh, ma'am. We will get your car looked at right away. I am sure we can work something out." (Backs away slowly.)

Me: "Can I use your phone?" … "Jay, can you pick me up?"

Jay: "Where are you?"

Me: "I am at the dealership." (I start crying again)

Jay: "I thought I told you we didn't have the money to get the car fixed, to wait."

Me: "Well...I prayed. God told me to bring it in."

Jay: "I will pick you up. Be there in 30 minutes."

Me: (Sigh.)

So, Jay picked me up and was not happy with me, to say the least. I didn't say much. Later that day, the dealership called and told us that it was $1,000, and we could break it up into three payments if we wanted. So, I thought that was a bit better.

It also happened to be Wednesday night, and we took the kids to Royal Rangers. I ran into the same business leader. He asked me about the van. I told him I took it in to get an estimate, and it was $1,000. He took out his checkbook and wrote me a check for the entire amount. When he handed it to me he said, "God told me to pay this bill for you the moment you told me you had the need, but not to give you the check until you stepped out in faith. Here you go."

I nearly fell out. It was such a great lesson for me and one I have never forgotten. God does care about your need, but He also cares about us growing in our faith and obeying Him. There may be someone waiting on you to take action and meet your need RIGHT NOW.

When I showed the check to Jay, he was nicely surprised and said, "Honey, I guess you did hear God. I'm sorry for not listening to you."

One of the things I always encourage people to do who have obstacles they are trying to solve is to ask God clearly what your next step should be. Not three steps ahead. Just one. Do the one thing, and you will get the next step provided. If you don't feel like you heard God lay anything on your heart, then just take a step that you think makes sense. You don't need the perfect financial plan, counselor, doctor, pastor of 60 years who you heard on the radio to do your marriage counseling for you. What you need is a good plan that you execute today on. Pray, write down what you hear God tell you, and then execute consistently.

The Word of God says that the just live by faith, and we cannot please God without it. Think about that as you pray and seek God for His perfect will. The perfect will of God requires that we stop operating out of our natural giftings and we rely on faith to fill in where we are weak. God's heart is always for our territory to be enlarged, and many times we have to be willing to get out of comfort zones even if that means you find out you missed the mark or things didn't end up like you thought they would.

Your Identity Work and Confession

Thank You, Jesus, You are the PIONEER and PERFECTOR of my faith, according to Philippians 1:6. You will perfect and finish the work You have begun in my heart and my calling. Thank You that because You overcame, I will not become weary or tired in my calling. I put my hope in You, and because of that Your promise is that I will rise up like the wings of eagles into my destiny. I will walk and not grow weary, according to Isaiah 40:31, because I hope in You and not in man.

I AM the JUST. I LIVE BY FAITH, according to Romans 1:17, and because of that I am pleasing to You. Illuminate to me by your Holy Spirit how to walk in faith in the places I see within my heart when I pray. I will not fear man, failure, or missing the mark of my high calling because I trust as I pray that You will make my way straight and even correct places I have wandered off because of Your great love for me.

Chapter 9
WHERE YOUR TRACK RECORD IS BUILT

"If everybody is thinking alike, then somebody isn't thinking."
– General George S. Patton

The great thing about Phase 3 is it reveals to you where your identity and authority have been solidified. It will also show you where you still need to dig into prayer at a deeper level and execute practically with boldness. One of the places where you might see a possible gap in your leadership is in the area of receiving and giving confrontation. This is because in order to see your vision fulfilled, you will have to be able to work consistently within a team environment. Teams require strong and secure leadership at the helm. The focus in this phase is learning how to see grace and truth released without unnecessary offense.

If you become defensive when people ask you to evaluate your results, then simply put, you're still operating from a fear-based mindset. This, in turn, will really hamper your ability to grow with grace. And you will stay stuck in this phase until you learn how to do this in a way that makes you a safe leader. This is because truly humble leaders are more concerned with discerning the will of God and the mission He is calling them to. Evaluating results is just part of that detached mission briefing! Again, if you evaluate from a military perspective on what worked and what didn't work, you are not so likely to take too much sabotage or success on yourself. The other point is, from a spiritual leadership perspective, you will know whether you can share the strategy with others or learn from your mistakes. You will be less worried about appearing to be "right" rather than just getting the best outcome you can out of strategic planning.

If you are in this place right now, your track record for future battles is being built, which is why it might feel like it's taking so long to be released at the level you're seeing internally. This is also why it's crucial you don't sabotage yourself by not being transparent with failures, yet still maintain an ability to communicate a clear, confident vision. Sometimes people will get hit with assignments of rejection in this phase that cause them to feel like they are not equipped to continue to lead or produce a greater vision. It could take on the form of people attempting to minimize your motives or reminding you of your past failures, but essentially, it's an attempt to erode your confidence so that you quit prematurely.

God never intends to disqualify us when we fail, rather He uses what causes us to cry out to Him for wisdom and strength to lead us to a greater place of humility. Some of what you may be experiencing right now is a simple refining on how to continue to serve others with grace and power when you feel emotionally overwhelmed.

It's one thing to feel internally weak or look back over your leadership and realize you really shouldn't have made that particular decision. It's another to become so flustered or dramatic when explaining how sorry you are that people become concerned about your ability to lead them. People maintain loyalty during crisis not because you do everything right but because you have built previous trust and can listen and integrate the best strategies during new pressure. If you cannot implement new strategies during new transitions, then you need to activate your faith because you're being victimized by doubt and unbelief. Here's why.

My soul hath them still in remembrance, and is humbled in me. This I recall to my mind, therefore have I hope. It is of the LORD'S mercies that we are not consumed, because his compassions fail not. They are new every morning; great is thy faithfulness. (Lamentations 3:20-23 KJV)

What you really find in this spiritual phase is the knowledge or teaching you have been assenting to won't be any kind of ground you can stand on during trials if you are not militantly applying it on a daily basis by faith. You cannot wait to test concepts and strategies during spiritual pressure, they must be executed on and implemented daily to create a robotic reaction during crisis.

This is also the place, if you are part of a team, where you will discover if the leaders are living behind the scenes what they teach publicly. The organizational beliefs posted on a website or the visionary culture repeated in the boardroom means little if during anxiety-ridden pressure it is not implemented. The heart of a leader is discovered not through charismatic preaching or motivational talks but through fiery pressure. This is where you really discover if the partners and leadership culture you are part of are living at a core level what they have been communicating.

What you say you believe in sunny skies means little. It's the beliefs and actions you execute during pain and storms that reveal your identity and how God has graced you to serve people. This is also why you can never put too much focus in emotional highs, bonding retreats, marketing projections, or anyone who wants to sell you how to build the ship who doesn't have three battleships out at sea already. Successful experiences that you can communicate clearly are what you use when you need to impart faith.

Remember what David said to Saul when he went up to slay the giant, and his ability to succeed was challenged?

"The Lord who delivered me from the paw of the lion and from the paw of the bear, He will deliver me from the hand of this Philistine." (1 Samuel 17:37)

This was not boasting. He was simply speaking directly to the spirit of fear in Saul that his identity was an overcomer, and this situation would be just like the rest. You can never reason with, patronize, or argue with fear. If you're doing this with people in your life right now, stop, because it's going to wear you out for what you need to focus on concerning the mission God has given you. You have to speak directly to people with fearful spirits and tell them exactly what's going to happen and then you execute quickly on what you said you were going to do.

You may find that identity statements you make will sometimes be misunderstood as pride. You will learn to recognize Christians who don't live in faith or rely on worldly wisdom and come to a place where their input or comments do not affect you AT ALL because you now recognize fear-based thinking. Your mission is to take on the battles that God has given you, and even now, you might be receiving an opportunity to take down a Goliath in your life.

Many times, people do not discern these faith-defining moments because they are masked in shame. They can cause you to shrink back from a fear of public outing if you fail.

Goliaths come when the clarity and outcome of a team identity are threatened and affect people inter-generationally. They typically result in demotion or promotion. A larger community is now getting a front seat view to your core beliefs. The best way to know if you are dealing with a Goliath moment in your life is the level of attention it draws to you alone. Goliaths typically require bold communication that force people into "fish or cut bait" moments.

Your reputation and core beliefs will be brought under a microscope and the results evaluated for all to see. Did you choose self-preservation, or did you make a decision for the good of the whole family or team? How did you respond during the pressure? Were you coachable or were you arrogant? Most of the time, from my personal experiences and watching this happen in hundreds of clients lives, there will be a financial stake in the battle at some point. Mammon is often revealed at these junctures.

Remember, when David slayed Goliath, his whole family was exempted from taxes and he was given the king's daughter as a reward! Imagine, the very brothers who were persecuting him now benefited from his courage. During Goliath moments in your life, you might experience tension from your family because you have pulled down tremendous idolatry! Walking in the spirit of God IS a force that makes people very uncomfortable. You need to see this as normal Christianity and not anything you are doing wrong. At the heart of Phase 3 is a refining on applying WHO YOU KNOW YOURSELF TO BE IN CHRIST to obstacles that now bring others into greater lordship or enable the status quo/idolatry.

This is also where people will attempt to label and intimidate you out of their own jealousy for the confidence you have gained from obeying God fully. You are becoming more fluid at being able to keep yourself faith-focused during oppression and maybe being given the opportunity to help others do the same. Activating faith for the future but not feeling compelled to entertain those you serve with worldly positive or motivational thinking. True spiritual leaders or messengers don't want to be "yes men or women" and they resist people-pleasing attempts. This is pressed down deeply into you during this phase.

It will all boil down to discerning the Holy Spirit's direction, obeying Him while attempting to keep unity as best you can. There will be times when that will not be possible, and people will need to be confronted or given consequences if the decisions they are choosing are harming the team's momentum and unity.

The next lesson that is being solidified is your ability to solve problems that affect the hearts and finances of others in a sacrificial way. When we make decisions that affect people's future hope and provision in a way that gives us the edge rather than benefiting them in a greater way, we are in danger of being manipulated by mammon. Whether you are in business or ministry, there will always be a way to build in a profitable way that enables you to give more than you receive.

If you are a woman, this is an extremely defining phase. It will force you to seek the Lord in a deeper way on who you believe He has called you to serve and how you will do this practically. What you have seen modeled that has been fruitful as opposed to what you have not seen be effective, will cause you to discover for yourself what you really believe about spiritual submission, roles, and leadership.

All of this wrestling before the Lord in prayer is what sets the foundation for your boldness. We are meant to carry spiritual authority in whatever realm we are serving in, whether it be business or ministry. This is also the phase where a lot of powerful calls are aborted. In the next chapter, I will be sharing more about how to truly recognize this and navigate it from a spiritual warfare perspective.

We have to be careful of defining people and their motives if we carry positional authority in the church because this can really destroy the calling of God on people's lives. When we label people, this is a form of witchcraft. I have been guilty of it, you have done it, but it needs to be repented of as it's not God's heart. We don't want a label to define people, even if their current choices substantiate that identity. Many times, people stay stuck in old identities just because they have a "tape" playing in their hearts and minds of a label someone they respected gave them at a weak point in time for them.

I have had more than a couple clients come to me who were told without proper testing that they were manic-depressed or mentally ill and handed three drugs. I have spoken to people personally who walked into a doctor's office and in five minutes were told they had ADHD and put on controlled substances. I am not saying there isn't a place for medication in some circumstances, but it is certainly not at the level that it is currently being promoted, and frankly, it opens up significant spiritual warfare for people.

As people of God, we want to speak life and break off ourselves and others definitions like alcoholic, stupid, lazy, selfish, mentally ill, depressed, womanizer, Jezebel, etc. We want only the Lord's identity to name and define us, our children, and our friends. It's important as soon as we realize we have done this to release ourselves and others from this. If people are unable to build new identities most of the time, it just boils down to getting militant enough in prayer, confession, and accountability to see the old wineskin pass away and the new one built.

You don't go into a new identity. You grow into one. Typically, it takes a year minimally after trust has been broken or you've had an epic failure for the new leadership to be solidified and the confidence gained. Don't delay your progress by "shoulding" on yourself.

I should be more mature. (Well, shouldn't we all?)

I should have known better. (Hindsight is always 20/20.)

I should have seen that coming. (Well, you won't miss it next time.)

Let's end this chapter by adding another confession to the places where your leadership might still need solidifying.

Your Identity Work and Confession

Father, in the name of Jesus, I declare over myself that no failure, rejection, or opinion of man will define me. Only You have the right to name me. Your Word says in Revelation 2 that as an overcomer You will give me a new name that only You and I shall know. I receive a spirit of holiness to sanctify and set me apart for the work of the ministry in my vocation. I humble myself before You and ask that You give me an ability to listen to ideas, thoughts, and strategies from others without feeling a need to fix myself. I ask You to give me wisdom to listen, thank the person for their input, and then tell them I will pray and think on what they have shared with me. I will then, O Lord, take their thoughts to You and allow You to correct and adjust me with GRACE and TRUTH. Everywhere I fail is a glory to You. Everywhere I succeed is a glory to You because all is done through Your name. I break off myself any curses, projections, or slander that has spoken over my future hope. I have a spirit of power, love, and a sound mind and have been anointed to make disciples for the kingdom of God according to Matthew 28. This is my mission, and it will continue until the day of my death and entrance into my heavenly reward. Give me increasing boldness, clarity, and strength to see the purposes and plans You have for me released on this earth.

Chapter 10
SABOTAGES FOR PIONEERS

"There's no quitting, I can't have quit in me. There was never an option to stop and quit."
— Lisa Jaster, third woman to graduate from U.S. Army Ranger School

I n the kingdom of God, your identity is to be an overcomer. We must be able on a given day to be receptive like Jesus was to ask and follow His Father's will (feminine in spirit) and assertive to push back demonic strongholds (which is typically more of a masculine trait). You cannot be either/or if you want to be an effective leader. This is because spiritual authority is not a gender or role. It's a position in the spirit realm that is created by understanding and applying your identity in Christ daily.

There also must be a tenacity and perseverance that do not make failure an option and that you believe you can carry both attributes with grace. Simply put, on any given day, you have to be able to be both masculine and feminine in spirit – in your vision, marriage, parenting, and servant leadership.

If you are always assertive and rarely receptive, you will struggle with exhaustion, harshness, impatience, frequent misunderstanding, and this every present feeling you never arrive. Always operating from passivity, you will find you share frequently about what you heard from God, resist the discipline it takes to produce your vision, be diluted with your boundaries, and constantly underestimate the force it takes to pull down demonic strongholds.

There needs to be a wonderful balance to becoming an overcomer in prayer, leading boldly, and multiplying your message. Jesus modeled this beautifully. His authority was carried naturally and unforced and because of this, people knew there was something different about Him. Why? Because when you operate out of your identity and God-given authority, what you do is just an extension of WHO you are. This is why other people's expectations and agendas for your life produce burdens and the ones that come from your prayer life and vision that God has given you are light to carry.

Supernaturally turning water into wine at a big party. Flipping tables aggressively to make a point to the religious establishment. Sweating blood to receive the cross, enduring with masculine energy having his skin flayed off, He exemplified perfect humility and perfect strength. Jesus spent time listening to His Father directionally (receptive), and then He executed boldly His identity and authority (assertively).

Remember, this is the part of the transition in your calling where you will begin to cause people to choose a fork in the road. You're moving from a visionary phase which is what you see internally (prophetically from listening to your Father's vision for your life) to more of an action-oriented (apostolic/modeling) place where you carry people in prayer and SHOW them the way to go through modeling. Because you're in a transition between unseen to actual practical results, you might feel this "dark soul" loneliness.

I see a couple things happen that contribute to the heaviness in this phase. One, clients have really worked hard to begin to grow their authority and because of this, they start outgrowing their old relationships who don't like the balance of power rearranged. Not that there should be that in a friendship but honestly, it can happen without intention. It could just be something as simple as you have built a relationship with someone who likes to feel needed. When you are more confident and taking bold action, guess what? If their identity was in feeling needed, they will not like your growth and will feel insecure. Most of the time, family or friends aren't going to realize they are struggling with jealousy, and you will get some passive-aggressive push back. That feeling that there is something going on, but you can't quite put your finger on it. This is because there has been an upset in power.

This happens with husbands and wives as well as close friends and business partnerships. When I hear this, I just encourage them to pray a blessing for the individual and also invite them into new things they are doing in order to help alleviate this disconnect. Remember, it's not your job to solve rejection for everyone; that's God's job. It's your opportunity to love them deeply, pray for them to be delivered, and let them take action so they break out of their own sabotaging patterns. You can't build a new identity for someone, and they won't do it without a struggle!

Another thing that happens is you're wearing your new identity awkwardly. If you haven't experienced a "suddenly" season before, it can be pretty uncomfortable. You might be a bit too enthusiastic to be around for people who are still dealing with feeling stuck. This is a point where as you gain more success, you need to be asking the Lord to give you a grace to recognize pride. Trust me, if you aren't asking God for grace beforehand, you will find yourself in a public setting where you will be embarrassed. The Holy Spirit has no problem outing boasting or selfish choices. Practically speaking, take the time once you begin to become more successful to ask for more accountability and give people who love you the chance to correct you before God does:).

As you grow influence, you will also have to grow in your transparency, humility, and willingness for others to put their fingers in your Kool-Aid. A sure sign of maturity in your life is when you get to the place where you ask your covenant friends who know you well for input into daily obstacles. You stop waiting for correction and you invite it. It's not about people pounding you to share or be needy, it's about you bowing deeper to Christ.

Without this level of authenticity, you are in danger of not having a wide spiritual covering when you begin to get tension for impacting in a greater way. If you are married, your spouse will be your main covering, but there is value in having other covenant relationships in your life to guard your integrity and help you identify attacks faster. Never sacrifice your time with covenant friends over "leadership responsibilities." Covenant friends are what keep you down to earth and will pray you though the worst demonic assaults.

Now let's talk briefly about the Jezebel spirit and specifically how some women are labeled with this for merely walking in their authority. I go into more detail in how to recognize this, deal with it, and move through it successfully with content I have called *Bold Spiritual Authority*, so we won't be going into this in-depth here, but I want to give you an overview of this as it is one of the primary attacks I see in this phase.

This is a label that is applied at times to women (or even sometimes men) who are undermining spiritual authority in the church, causing division, or using sexual manipulation against pastors, worship leaders, or elders. All of that sounds rather "out there," so let's talk about what specific results you will see if you're really dealing with this in your spiritual or professional life. You don't hear about this outside the church, but I have walked many professional and corporate clients through this in their company culture.

First, you're going to immediately become double-minded and anxious out of your character. When I have a client who is attempting to set boundaries and lead boldly, and they feel undermined and confused in speaking to someone who is challenging their mindsets, I begin to pray a spiritual covering over them. Leaders who are dealing with this spirit behind a person's actions will feel uncharacteristically double-minded.

This spirit thrives on passivity and your attempts to be kind or a peace-maker. It despises divine and ordered authority or teaming. It's passive-aggressive, conducive to rage, and its agenda is ultimately to take the leadership reins in an organization or partnership. Outside the church, this spirit will attempt to undermine the authority of anyone who seeks to change the culture from being undisciplined or sexually-charged to a professional, service-based leadership. If they are already entrenched when you arrive into the workplace, this spirit will attempt to intimidate you if you make any changes that challenge the idolatry that is in place. It loves to have a workplace setting full of coarse joking and over-drinking, and will shame you if they cannot intimidate you and elevate their own personal agenda to the hurt of others.

This is because people who are really being manipulated by this spirit are trying to replace the pure worship of God and unity (within a team) with the all-about-me "self-glorifying message." Within the church, the pastor, prayer leaders, and worship leaders are primary targets for this spirit, as these three giftings pioneer in unity to honor and lift up the name of Christ. In the church, this spirit will thrive when people are prophesying and personal kingdom building but not equipping or releasing in humility. Personal kingdom building is all about building a one man show. To equip, train, and release people into their own visions, you have to have a heart for other people's success, not just your own. It also invites order, accountability, and transparency.

Personally, I have seen from a coaching perspective, some of what people label a Jezebel spirit can be narcissism that has gone unchecked because the individual lacked or resisted true accountability. Or they haven't sought healing for emotional wounds. Jezebels don't repent or seek a solution to their problems. They want to be right and they have a mindset of victimization they really don't want to resolve. They also rarely have a positive track record with teams.

Let's talk about what does not make you a Jezebel:

1. Assertively asking people who are in leadership to be professional and do the things that are consistent with the identity they are communicating. Executing on what you say you're going to do is part of your job as a CEO or pastor or leader in your home. If asking you when you're going to get things done offends you, you need to grow in your leadership.

2. Politely disagreeing with the direction of the leadership. Communicating a better way or suggesting an alternative route is not rebellious. It's a sign you have a confident, smart team around you.

The good news is most of the time, if this is addressed early in a church or work environment, people who just haven't been trained to work in a team environment or who are socially awkward, can have the opportunity to experience authentic community where they can be delivered, healed, and RELEASED into more of their purpose. What is important to remember is that we have been redeemed by Christ to take back what the enemy has stolen from people. That requires us to love forcefully, confront early, and give people an opportunity to take ownership of their behavior before demoting them or outing them. God does not correct publicly before He corrects privately or with two people.

Here is one prayer to help you avoid sabotage you will receive from your pioneering and build success.

Your Identity Work and Confession

Father, in the name of Jesus, Your Word says that I can do all things through Christ that strengthens me. (Philippians 4:13) I can overcome all offense, all betrayal, all disappointment, and all persecution because You endured all of it, and I am within You. (Matthew 6:12) Give me grace to love people militantly as You loved them – freely, practically, unconditionally, and not expecting anything in return. (Luke 6:27) Let all men know I am a disciple by the way I choose to honor others above myself. I declare over my life and leadership that I will walk in a spirit of power, love, and a sound mind. Today, I ask You, Holy Spirit, to help me listen and respond to You internally in the secret place of my heart. I ask You, Lord Jesus, to give me discernment to pull down idolatry in my life and warn others in a spirit of love. Let me know when to listen and when to confront the truth in love in all boldness. (Matthew 16:23) It is my desire to walk in grace and truth.

Give me divine opportunities to share my testimony and teach! (Matthew 28) I will cast out demons today and I will walk in signs and wonders. Greater works shall I do because Your mission is my mission today – to make disciples and see Your kingdom advanced!

Chapter 11
THE TEST OF COMMITMENT

"It is fatal to enter a war without the will to win it."
– General Douglas MacArthur

You are now entering the fourth level of spiritual warfare. It comes to test the commitment you have to the call of God and your willingness to pay the price for the freedom of others. It's not about you anymore, but the people God is calling you to serve. For their sake and reaching them, this phase requires strategic work and laser focus.

In this phase, you're being commissioned to teach and impact others through preaching, speaking, and writing – the mechanisms that will lead to exponential multiplication. You now are going to receive the opportunity to do the work to begin to multiply the message God has given you.

The aim in this phase is to subdue the whole earth (Genesis 1:28) with the transformational love of Christ (your story of how

Christ set you free). This will require you to think in terms now of teams, technology, systems, and platforms. Very unspiritual feeling but necessary for you to expand with grace.

Avoiding dualistic thinking in this phase is very important. In other words, when you pray, serve, and talk about Jesus, that's spiritual! When you have to write, speak, market, and create systems for reaching those people, that's unspiritual! Don't sabotage the mission God has given you by separating your spiritual life and work into little boxes. When we are in Christ, everything we do is consecrated, sanctified and set apart, or here's the truth, you don't truly believe you are abiding in Christ. There should be no separation between secular and sacred. If your focus is to see people transformed for the kingdom when you get up every day, then you're in the ministry.

Multiplication will require something of you from a stewardship perspective. Someone had to catch, wash, and bring the fish to the feeding of the 5,000. Jesus didn't just "poof" fish up in a basket. God uses what we bring to Him in faith. It's hard work calling about venues, fund-raising, marketing, and building a platform for your God-given message, but if your heart is to glorify God and not yourself, this can be done with grace.

I love what A. Larry Ross, Billy Graham's personal press secretary for over 34 years, shared about his integrity before men and God. Graham never sacrificed the long-term viability of his ministry for the short-term visibility of media publicity and promotion. Rather, he understood and cultivated the character and calling that came with his station. He sought platforms for his message, not publicity for his ministry, to communicate biblical truth beyond audiences that attended his crusades.

In order to focus on platforms for your message rather than publicity, you will need to be very clear on your core values and boundaries that you create as you communicate your message.

The road is riddled with women and men in spiritual leadership who made one or two poor decisions, lost the mantle God had given them, and then were defined by these choices for the rest of their lives. One of the ways that you avoid unnecessary spiritual warfare that goes with Phase 4 is to hold yourself to a higher standard than you expect from others.

Core values, courage, and commitment will define how you think and fight in Phase 4. You must be confident not just in your ability to serve, but you must be confident in those you choose to partner with. In chaos, character matters, which is why if you are in this phase you want to take the time to break down practically your core values into practical strategies for yourself and those around you that you lead. These have to be communicated and held to militantly.

The spiritual warfare that comes against you in this phase is related to the results you are producing in others, therefore you must be prepared for the sabotages the enemy seeks to create for you ahead of time.

At the beginning of Phase 4 in my life, I was coming out of a season where there was tremendous emotional pain in my closest relationships. I would say my heart was traumatized. I had been deeply disappointed by multiple people in our lives that I thought were shepherding our family, only to find out after a long period of investing relationally, that was not the case.

It was the worst of times but also the greatest defining moments I have learned as a leader. I look back and just thank God now that in His sovereignty He did the pruning work He did in my life as without it, I would have never been doing what I am today. However, as I began to seek God for a heart-healing, I knew clearly I was to quit my lucrative sales job, resign from my ministry position in the church, and rest spiritually as God wanted to do a new thing in me.

As I obeyed, God began to drop down a new vision in my heart for the next couple decades. None of this clarity however was released to me until I obeyed Him in resigning the positions I currently had. Note to self: If you want God to do a new thing, you have to be willing to let go of your old identity no matter how practical or prosperous it seems in the natural.

During a significant pivot point in our spiritual and family lives, the mission focus we were invested in came to an abrupt end. Jay and I had to go back to the Lord and ask Him how we were to continue to carry out that vision in our own lives. We hadn't moved away from our family, uprooted our children, and changed jobs just to have the whole vision die. When God drops down WHO you are and WHERE He is sending you, it may change forms, but it doesn't end because your mission focus is the weakness and yet gifting God has formed in you.

This same year, as I resigned all my positions, I experienced an identity theft for almost a million dollars. I mean who has back-to-back deep disappointment for one straight year and then an ID theft for a million dollars. People get their purse stolen, not an identity theft so large the FBI has to get involved. Every part of my life was getting dismantled. It was an epic chaotic move on the enemy's part, and at the same time, while I sat in the FBI's local Atlanta office as they handed me their card (in case I got pulled over by the police for impersonating myself), it finally hit me that Satan was trying to abort some kind of powerful shift that was coming for me. It will be the same for you. When you are reaching a point of really stepping into the next authority and identity God has for you, you will go through huge second-guessing again in another round of trials. I have seen it in my own life and that of hundreds of clients again and again. Here's what you need to understand and take comfort in as you enter Phase 4. It's normal for them to be created in the middle of chaos.

God is not confined by confusion, voids, or oppression. He also does not save by many but rather by winnowing down resources in the midst of great pressure, so He is glorified. He is the light within us so that means we can always at any point, whether we feel like we have a perfect or clear plan, receive the clarity to move into a new identity and season through Christ if we stay faith filled.

This is why if you are in this place right now, you must be activating your faith in the morning every day, declaring who you are in Christ, where you're going as best as it has been revealed to you, and thanking God for the provision you need to get to the people God is sending you to!

Let me repeat that again. God is faithful. He loves drama, chaos, and voids. We can always move into a new identity, authority, and power and receive the resources if we are faith filled and willing to stand through fear. Don't allow the enemy to starve you out of your joy and purpose from the fear of lack of resources.

After I got through the initial heart trauma of that year, I happened to launch at the beginning of 2007 and the second worst financial climate since the Great Depression. I was tempted with another form of identity theft as I launched my business. I was encouraged by other business coaches to create a "fake persona" under the guise of appearing more successful than I was at the time. Hyping my numbers, exaggerating my results. Anytime you are in a new move of God, and you don't have enough experience, the enemy attempts to cause you to strive rather than trust. When you strive, you're in danger of reverting to self-sabotaging behaviors you have learned in order to survive. I knew this could really take me in an old cycle I had already broken out of.

I was surrounded by business leaders who encouraged me to "fake it till I made it" with New Age mantras and visualization techniques. The problem with that is, to me, it smacked of idolatry, self-promotion, and a lack of authenticity. I was invited to many events by coaches that claimed to be Christians, but at the center of the coaching was a spirit of mammon. It was hugely frustrating to me. I wanted to get paid to help people receive transformation, but my focus wasn't to squeeze every dime I could get out of the client. My aim was to serve powerfully, have God at the center so He received the glory, and grow profitably. Essentially, there was this underlying tension during the first year to compromise on my core values. I solved that, and you can, too, by becoming very clear about what you will do, what you won't do, and keeping a very tight circle of trusted partners.

When Billy Graham's influence began to grow, so did the temptation to compromise. He solved this by creating what is known in ministry circles as the "Modesto Manifesto." It helped him avoid allegations of impropriety concerning money, sex, and power. For example, one of Billy Graham's core values was to operate with financial transparency. This meant he communicated clearly to his team and to the audiences he spoke to that every dime of their offering went to furthering the platform, not going into his personal pocket. To combat any suspicion of impropriety financially, he took a salary from his board rather than dip into any of the offerings.

Here are the four strategies he created with his team that guided their day to day operations and choices.

- Operate with financial transparency.
- Never travel or be alone with the opposite sex.
- Avoid criticizing other pastors or churches.
- Be honest with publicity and numbers. No hype.

I felt relieved to have discovered the issue I was struggling with other people had solved by just breaking down how your core values translate practically. For example, Chick-fil-A has a core value of honoring God on Sundays and allowing all their employees to rest and attend church. Practically speaking, they give everyone that day off, and that's an expectation that has permeated the company culture. However, imagine if the CEO required everyone in his organization to take off on Sunday, and then personally stayed home and did paperwork on Sunday. This kind of sabotage happens every day, and it creates a huge hole in your identity as well as eroding the trust of those around you.

A personal, family, or corporate core value that is created, stated, and then not enforced is not just spiritual warfare, it's a failure in leadership. Depending on the severity of the breach, it can cause slight disconnect or severe relational damage. From an anointing perspective, a lack of authenticity and integrity lifts the mantle of power on your life, so this is one of those areas of leadership you want to get right.

Basically, all your boundaries and strategies should be to protect you and/or your team from accusation and love other people deeper. Your boundaries might be tighter depending on the message you are bringing but essentially, as you grow more successful you will want to guard your calling. Remember, the only people who have a problem with core values and respecting boundaries are the people that don't have any or aren't adhering to their own because they are people-pleasers.

Take the time to break down your core values into practical and tangible actions, and you will find it's much easier to stay committed to do the right thing than be tempted to do the wrong thing in your ministry or business.

In Phase 4, you are moving from a place of individual security to providing larger amounts of people with tangible transformation. This will require you to be more disciplined with your thoughts, time, and actions. There is no glorification of Christ without suffering or sacrifice. This has nothing to do with your salvation or whether you are in business or ministry, but rather equipping you to understand that there is a price you must be willing to invest in to serve the people God is calling you to.

Here are some steps I would suggest that you integrate into your identity if you want to walk in a demonstration of power on your life. To be anointed means you have been graced to serve in a very specific way and with tangible power. You have been willing to stay disciplined and *obey God in the tests* He has given you. Here's what I want you to know about the anointing as I have seen God equip me practically to stay focused, endure testing and trials, and stay faithful.

1. You cannot carry an anointing of God on your life if you are not a man/woman who knows the Word of God, worships God weekly, and lives a life of prayer. You can be excellent at what you do but you cannot carry an anointing of God that breaks demonic strongholds. That's what the anointing is for. It's a force that confronts darkness, breaks wrong mindsets, and sets people free.

2. Testing to carry the anointing is different than what the Bible describes as trials. Trials refine our faith and come to all Christians. The anointing is an invitation given by God in a particular season of your life that is to affirm and give you a boldness in order to SEND YOU as a messenger. For example, Jesus was called into the wilderness to be tried. The apostles were told to pray and wait for the baptism of the Holy Spirit, so they could carry the anointing on them as they were being sent to pioneer the church.

3. If you want to prepare yourself to carry the anointing, you must be willing to begin to seek God for it, become a disciplined person with your time and your body, and start building a team.

In the last chapter, we will be talking about how you can create your boldest identity zones and exactly WHO God is calling you to serve specifically. God is not calling you to disciple everyone and set EVERYONE free contrary to what you may have been thinking! He is anointing you to serve a certain segment of people who you will have authority with because you have overcome in that area or God has opened a door by His grace to be sent there. Let's end with this identity prayer for Phase 4.

Your Identity Work and Confession

Thank You, Father God, that the love of Christ was manifested in me because You sent Christ, and He lives and abides within my heart. (1 John 4:9) For this reason and Your glory, I declare Acts 1:8 over myself today, that I have received power from the Holy Spirit because I believe, and I will be a witness in the places and to the people You are calling me to set free. I want to thank You that You are appointing me and anointing me to preach, teach, and cast out devils. I am responding to the call of God on my life, and I will build a team according to Luke 10:1-2 to guard my calling and help me stay effective. The harvest is plentiful, Lord. I am thanking You, Lord, for sending me! As I worship and fast, You will send people to pray for me and set me apart for the work which you have called me. (Acts 13:2-3)

Chapter 12
RESOLVE AND RESULTS

"Hardness,' I was learning, was the supreme virtue among recon Marines. The greatest compliment one could pay to another was to say he was hard. Hardness wasn't toughness, nor was it courage, although both were part of it. Hardness was the ability to face an overwhelming situation with aplomb, smile calmly at it, and then triumph through sheer professional pride."
— *Nathaniel Fick,* One Bullet Away: The Making of a Marine Officer

In Phase 4, you will experience another round of second-guessing. This will be compounded by how much you have to learn to discover your boldest identity zones and WHO God is sending you to serve. You will have to have great resolve to resist internalizing lack and oppression as your identity.

Identity is talked about a lot in Christian circles from the perspective of WHO you are in Christ as well as in the business realm from a branding perspective. But let me tell you what that looks like spiritually and practically in your vision first from a faith-based perspective. Unless you build this first in your own personal leadership, you are borrowing someone else's identity and/or brand, which leaves you in a position where you won't have as much kingdom boldness.

This is different for every person, but here is an example from my life.

I'm living authentically with the people I am accountable to steward relationally, starting with my husband, family, and close-friends.

I have a vision that I have asked God to download to me full of His purposes.

I am applying myself daily to say "no" to the things that are outside of my vision and "yes" to the things that are in it. I want to be led by the Holy Spirit to be flexible if necessary, but not distracted and frustrated.

And here's another thing about the process you may find yourself in as you move into a launching phase for business or ministry. It's normal for your testimony and the strategies you have to learn to succeed to be created in the middle of chaos.

He is the light within us, so that means we can always at any point, whether we feel like we have a perfect or clear plan, move into serving people by discipling, coaching, training, or speaking. Let me repeat that again. We can always move into a new identity with new authority and receive the resources if we are faith filled and willing to stand through our own insecurity. Why? Because it is no longer about us, but the people God is calling us to serve, and He will empower you by the Holy Spirit to be for others what they need.

Again, here is a practical example to encourage you. Remember, we walk by faith and not by sight.

I grew up in an alcoholic home, decided to major in Criminology in college, and then launched into homeschooling, though I had no teaching experience.

Jay and I sold our home in Tallahassee, left all our family to church plant with a team to Atlanta with no experience in ministry.

After Jay experienced a lay-off and we tapped our savings, he asked me to go to work for a sales company, and I had no experience in business. (I made the top sales team in eight months.)

Experienced an identity theft for a million dollars when we were stabling out financially. Because of this, I was asked to do a TV commercial for a national identity theft company with no experience speaking. I moved forward, and this turned into getting paid to become a spokesperson for them.

Started running to decompress from this and other things that were stressing me and finished a half and full marathon in one year with no experience as a runner.

Pioneered my own successful international coaching company right at the beginning of the second worst recession since the Depression with ZERO money and no marketing experience. Grew it from nothing after I was told by bunches of "Master Level" coaches I would never be successful building a brand out of my own identity and message. Developed four coaching systems, three teams, developed my own workshops training, and all of this with no business or seminary experience.

So, I can tell you a thing a two about creating new successful identities if you feel like God has called you to do ministry through your business. And if you're like me, you have no experience or "business sense," I want to encourage you that you don't have to have a ton of it. What you need is to be good at stewarding people's hearts and staying consistent to serve until you can build your expertise and credibility.

So, when you are given the OPPORTUNITY for an identity shift or to serve from a biblical point of view, it's typically hidden in the midst of loss, hiding, and chaotic atmospheres. Every giant of the faith biblically had to move forward with nothing but God sending them a challenge or giving them a simple invitation. Think Moses, Gideon, Barak, David, Saul on the road to Damascus, Peter, Paul....

You will only receive an invitation or strategy for the one next step. You will absolutely NOT receive the whole plan and what the new identity will mean for you. It will be RISKY if it's God, typically! So many people hold back at this point, trying to work out of their intellectual realm or plan it out financially. Identity shifts are NOT logical, they are divinely orchestrated.

The invitation will have to be accepted and you will have to step out in faith. You will have to pay a cost financially or in the form of tension in your current relationships. Sometimes both. This is to bring you to place of dependence on God, so He can define your identity in a deeper way. You will have to let go of old support to receive the new people God will bring to you.

Secondly, a new identity means you are going to receive more authority and influence, IF you keep your leadership model tight, take full ownership for where mistakes have been made, and you keep moving forward in who God has called you to serve.

This is where many people don't make the transition. They compromise on the core values that got them to the shift because tension and spiritual warfare come to test your new authority. Your leadership model is what you put into place daily in order to keep you focused and processing stress so you can keep growing.

The bottom line is new identities are created inwardly first in your inner man through prayer. Then when you agree with WHO God is calling you to become so He can use you as He desires to, you begin to be given the strategies on a practical level in order to move to an expert status.

Essentially what we are talking about is pioneering, and here's the thing – it's not for everyone. There is a cost you will pay to see lives impacted for the kingdom and to be released into your calling. Becoming a bold leader also means you're going to have to take a stand when others are wishy-washy on their opinions. Also, that you aren't waiting for people to open the door for you, but you're doing the work to get in front of the people God is calling you to.

Stepping into your boldest identity zones from a Christian perspective starts with you being willing to serve from a place of transparency and weakness. I do very little gifting analysis in my business, but rather I look for the places in people's lives where they are either hiding from God and need to yield (because this is potential power point when they overcome in this area) or the places they have already pulled down strongholds and built a testimony. This is their boldest identity zone! The place where they have been tested or divinely positioned and what did God did through them during that process. When you operate out of this grace, you are now positioning yourself to have apostolic power flowing through your business.

Everyone has a particular niche or people that God sends them to. For example, what did the Apostle Paul say to the Ephesians? Paul, an apostle of Christ Jesus through the will of God, to the saints that are at Ephesus, and the faithful in Christ Jesus. He knew exactly who the Lord was giving him authority to serve. The saints in Ephesus and also other Christians who were faithful.

Here's how I crafted that for my own prayer purposes and client messaging:

Becky, an identity coach through the will of God, to those who join my Leadership Team, read my books, and other men and women I am asked to speak to.

How can I be so confident that it is the will of God for me to coach and that I have authority to set people free? Because first of all I was doing this through my identity in Christ before I ever launched a business. I started with my family, friends, neighbors, and those God put in my path. I built a track record of stewardship and then at a certain point I channeled that into a model that I could scale into a larger business.

The biggest thing I want you to know today is you won't have confirmation through client testimonials when you initially launch. You have to know before God that He has called you and move forward with the courage into establishing your vision. Most Christians just get stuck on this first step because they keep waiting on God to open some kind of door for ministry, speaking, writing, or coaching. They say things like, "If it's God's will, people will invite me." This doesn't always happen. What does is your gifting, diligence, perseverance, and resolve make a way for your message to be shared, and people are transformed, and you receive favor.

Your vision won't grow because you love God. There are many people who love God and are faithful to Him but have stagnate businesses and ministries. It will grow because you discover what specific results you can produce for people, and they will invest with you to receive that same breakthrough. You have to cultivate a strong work ethic that does not quit and solves obstacles quickly.

You can call it an anointing (and I believe that is accurate and/or you can call it hard work to identify WHO you're called to!). So, the faith and courage are what launch you out into your calling. The business and branding work is what makes you grow consistently.

As you do this faithfully, you are now positioned to multiply your message. On a side note, this is often where you get *greater spiritual warfare* because you are impacting lives for Christ through your leadership and service.

These are all steps that are necessary for you to take if you are going to want to get paid as a Christian speaker, coach, writer, or minister.

Narrow Down Your Boldest Identity Zones

What subjects could I teach on with passion and enthusiasm out of the pain or crisis I have been in? When you begin to talk about this subject, do people sit up and pay attention? Write down five to ten topics that you could talk about passionately. Circle your top three in red as possible bold identity zones. You want to narrow yourself down to three and stay focused on these. Are these three zones ones that you could spend 15 to 45 minutes a day acquiring more knowledge in, investing money into growing, and developing content around? If you can answer "yes" to this and you're willing to do the work to move into being an expert in that realm, move forward into the next step.

Identify Who You Get Great Results With

Who specifically do I get the BEST results with? Male or female? Professional? Entrepreneurs? High performance people? What is their approximate age? Where do they live? Are they single? Married? What do they do for fun? What causes do they give to? What kind of clubs do they belong to? Where do they vacation? Where do they go to church? How do they spend money?

Identify Who You Don't Want to Work With

This is important. I decided I was going to have a screen system for all incoming clients. I wasn't going to do a "free" session, and I wasn't going to work with people who weren't ready to take immediate action. I didn't want to be a counselor, or I would have gone to school for that. I wanted to activate people's faith and help them get breakthrough! So, I set up a screening system with them with ten questions they had to answer in detail before I would meet with them. It automatically did two things for me. First, it winnowed out the people who just wanted to complain or "pick my brain" with no intention of hiring me. Number two, it helped me ask them the questions that I knew would give them the most momentum and reveal their pain. People don't seek solutions or stay consistent until you can help them clarify the pain level they are in and what you can do to eliminate that for them.

Identify Your Strengths

Ask yourself the following question: What do I love to talk about or do that will set me apart from my competition? Your goal for this step is to find out your "bold zone" that people will recognize is unique about you and that you will even get referrals for. Bold prayer is this zone for me. It set me apart naturally as it was something that was a very strong part of my identity. I also had a lot of experience overcoming mindsets that were developed from growing up in a fear-based, addiction-based home, so people began to send me their family and friends who fit this description. People knew I would fast as well as pray if I had to in order to see them successful. I want to encourage you to not worry about mixing "God" and your business. Focus on being you. If you pray with people all the time, then why not do that in your business?

Do the Work to Build Credibility

When you are an unknown figure and have no established platform such as television, radio, or a book you have published, you have to create it yourself. The easiest way to do this is through a website, weekly and monthly service offerings, building a list, and creating products so that you develop name brand recognition. What happens eventually is by being faithful to steward all of this, your circle of influence is enlarged, and you are possibly given an open door with the media or larger audiences.

The bottom line is your core identity and what you want to accomplish mission-wise for your audience is what your brand rotates around. WHO YOU are and what you want to produce in their lives. Your business brand is just an extension of who you are in your personal life. The tighter identity work you do in your personal leadership, the better your branding clarity will be.

How Can You Make Your Speaking or Coaching Affordable for Everyone?

When you begin, create a $20.00 product, then a $99.00 product, and then lastly a bigger package that people can invest into. You want to be able to provide coaching at various financial levels. What will your price range be and what exactly can you provide in an over-the-top way to ensure you are going to be talked about and referred in a great way?

Lastly, I want to remind you that the work I am asking you to do will feel very "unspiritual." You may also struggle still with a lack of clarity and confidence. This is normal for everyone who pioneers. Be willing to do a crappy job and don't let perfectionism hold you back. You're going to be fuzzy mentally on some days or just anxious and have to push yourself through in faith. This is all normal tension. Financial hardship is part of all new endeavors. God will give you grace to hold on long enough until your confidence is built if you just don't quit! I know this may not seem like very good business advice, but you can't associate worldly success with creating a spiritual/purposed calling or even a significant life. Doing what you love for a living will require you to make a lot of sacrifices.

I can tell you that not one time have I looked back and regretted any financial decisions I made to do what I am doing for a living. Weekly, I receive emails, Facebook, and Instagram messages telling me that my strategies have transformed people's lives. I am just telling you that when you begin to hear that your LIFE is making that level of difference for someone who has struggled for decades with no hope, you will do whatever it takes to stay on track.

Let's end by helping you create as big a vision as you can create right now. Ten years ago, I wrote that my dream was to have a profitable coaching business that changes lives for Christ that I ran from a home in the country with my horses. I am now living that dream.

Write out where you live.

Write out who is with you.

Write out what your schedule will be and what the home looks like.

Write what you are doing for people weekly.

Write out who you will give your extra money to that you make.

My friend, hang on through all the spiritual warfare! My vision came to pass and so will yours if you don't quit! Pray strong. Be bold in your leadership and multiply your message for Christ!

Here is your last identity prayer for Phase 4!

Your Identity Work and Confession

Lord Jesus, thank You, we do not wrestle against flesh and blood, but against principalities, against powers, against the rulers of the darkness of this age, against spiritual hosts of wickedness in the heavenly places. (Ephesians 6:12) Father, in the name of Jesus, I ask You to give me a bulldog tenacity. I declare I will not bow the knee to lack in my business or ministry. I will wrestle with the authority You have given me for the high calling of transforming lives for Your kingdom. I will prosper according to Your will and timing, and I thank You that you desire me to be in health and prosper in everything I do so I can be sent to be a blessing.

I AM the righteousness of Christ as a coach. (Romans 10:5-6)

I AM anointed to teach, preach, cast out demons, and heal in the name of Jesus. (Luke 4:18)

I AM able to overcome all affliction, tribulation, and oppression, because greater is He that is in me than he that is in the world. (1 John 4:4)

ABOUT THE AUTHOR

Becky Harmon lives in the metropolitan of White, Georgia (est. population 800) with her husband, Jay, 2 horses, 2 dogs, and 2 cats that leaped out of tree to be rescued as they knew she was *clearly* an animal lover. She has been married to her husband, Jay, affectionately known as "Superman" for over thirty years and is the mother of four adult children – Wes, Josh, Abby, and Joseph. She loves teaching people how to use the Word of God to battle strongholds and build an identity of an overcomer. In her spare time, she enjoys being outdoors, hiking, riding her horses, and gardening.

For more information on how Becky can help your organization activate and train Messengers for Christ, contact her at www.successnotsabotage.com.

REFERENCES

Chapter 1:
Woititz, Janet Geringer. "13 Characteristics." Excerpt from *Adult Children of Alcoholics – The Expanded Edition*. Pompano Beach, FL: Health Communications, 1983.

Chapter 4:
Seamands, David. *Freedom from the Performance Trap*. Victor Books, 1991.

Chapter 11:
Graham, Billy. (2016, October 24). "The Modesto Manifesto: A Declaration of Biblical Integrity." Retrieved from https://billygraham.org/story/51705/.

CPSIA information can be obtained
at www.ICGtesting.com
Printed in the USA
LVOW13s0430160718
583889LV00014B/468/P